THE GIFT IN YOU

discover **new life** through
gifts hidden in your mind

dr. caroline leaf

For further information please contact
Dr. Caroline Leaf by visiting www.drleaf.net
or write to the office of Dr. Leaf.

2140 E Southlake Blvd.
Suite L #809
Southlake, TX 76092

Distributed by Thomas Nelson Publishers,
printed in the United States of America.

Disclaimer: The information and solutions offered in this book are intended
to serve as guidelines for managing toxic thoughts, emotions and bodies.
Please discuss specific symptoms and medical conditions with your doctor.

Inprov, Ltd. with licensing permission from Switch On Your Brain USA LP

DEDICATION

To Jesus Christ, my Lord and Savior,

Who has given me the privilege of showing the world that every person is uniquely gifted with a special piece of eternity.

To my beloved husband and children,

Who have given their love and support and helped me rewire my "gift-blockers." I couldn't have done it without you.

To all of you out there,

I believe that everyone is gifted; I see this in my husband, my children, my clients and even in myself. I celebrate the fact that all mankind can think and learn – it is a magnificent gift from our Creator and a gift to be used with joy. It is my desire that you will use your brains and not be scared to say, "I have done well."

TABLE OF CONTENTS

PART ONE: The Gift in You

INTRODUCTION

What is your gift?

What do you have inside of you that no one else has?

Maybe no one ever told you that you have a gift.

Maybe you've been told over and over that you have a special gift but haven't really been able to believe it.

Maybe you have discovered your particular gift but haven't been living or growing in it to the greatest potential.

Many people never uncover their gifts, which is a tragedy.

You have a divinely pre-wired gift – a gift God has placed within you – and in that gift you have everything you need to achieve your unique and marvelous purpose.

You can discover what your gift is and, by learning its structure, begin to thrive in it.

Over twenty years ago, when I first started researching the science of thought, I could not have predicted that the science of neurons, dendrites and cells could help unlock potential, giftings and freedom. That's why I'm so passionate about the science of thought.

Understanding how our gifts are structured is just the beginning, but once we start the process, we launch out into a lifetime of lasting change.Your purpose is to live beyond yourself, but you can't share your gift if it's hidden. You can't live in your purpose if you aren't operating in your gift. You can't grow into your God-ordained self if your gift is blocked.

In Part Two, the Gift Profile, the 210-question journey will help you gain a better understanding of *how* you are uniquely gifted and how your gift is structured.

In Part Three, you will learn how to live out your gift.

Exploring the twelve gift-blockers in Part Four will help you recognize what might be standing in your way of operating fully in your gift.

But first let's look closely at the science of thought – how your brain really works and why your gifting might surprise you.

1

CHAPTER ONE:
{UNCOVERING YOUR HIDDEN GIFT}

"I knew you before I formed you in your mother's womb"
(Jeremiah 1:5 NLT).

Your gift is the missing piece. It's always an answer and never a problem. It is unique, intentional, having a purpose, design and measurable structure.

Since we all crave to be accepted and welcomed, sometimes we compare our gifts to others', attempting to measure if we belong; but that's like trying to reshape your fingerprint to match someone else's – impossible.

When you read about someone else's accomplishments and adopt his or her roadmap as your own, you will limit where your gift can take *you*. You can only be you. Who you are at the core will leak out, no matter how much you suppress it. In God's truth, the true you is meant to glorify, to love, to reach beyond yourself, but you cannot grow into the fullest expression of God's creation if you live in doubt or unrest, if you constantly undermine your gift by trying to copy other people's.

In order to sustain a consistent outlook and pattern, your thoughts, your words, your spirit and your actions must line up. That means when you say something that your brain doesn't "believe" – if your statement isn't part of you on a cellular level – it is unsustainable.

Neurologically, you are not wired for someone else's gift. You can try as hard as you want. You can listen to as many teachings as you possibly can. You can buy all the books with an instant formula for a business mogul's success. You can adopt all of the popular motivational sayings. But even then, you will never have someone else's gift.

Your own gift is *more* than enough, and once you uncover that gift and its structure, you can walk in freedom, knowing yours is unlike anyone else's.

Your life experiences, the lessons you've learned, and your unique gift all combine, giving you the opportunity to walk into the future with unlimited potential to grow into your own success.

Success isn't defined by a collection of assets, an accumulation of power or cash in the bank. If that were the formula, there would be no sorrow for those in the highest tax brackets. Rather, success is living out God's purpose for your life – using the gifting He has given – and every single one of us will express it differently, because every single one of us can do something that someone else can't.

Once, I was halfway through a training session for a group of teachers in Eastern Cape, South Africa, when this really came alive for me in a profound way.

We all know teachers hold tremendous responsibility in their hands to help children grow in their potential. They are unrecognized warriors, often facing tremendous obstacles. This particular group of teachers was facing quite a difficult task – equipping children who had very few resources, under quite stressful circumstances.

One teacher, feeling the strain of his situation said, "Dr. Leaf, you've got it all wrong. There's a child in my class who's so stupid, there's no way he has a gift." Well, for once in my life, I was dumbstruck.

Then, one of his colleagues stepped in and countered, "Do you know what, sir?" For a moment, I held my breath because I knew we would soon learn if the material from the seminar was sinking in or if we should duck for cover. Thankfully, this teacher had embraced the core of the importance of living in our gifting. He countered, "That child – that so-called stupid child – can do something that you can't do." And it is true.

Each person can do something no one else can do. There's something each child can do that no one else can do.

Use the Gift Profile in Part Two as an opportunity to find it. Find it in yourself. Find it in your children. Find it in your spouse. Find it in your colleagues at work. Find it, because in it you will also find the truth of God's living promises.

You were not built to struggle. Your brain is wired to function according to a specific sequence. When you discover that sequence, that structure, you unlock great potential.

CHAPTER TWO:
{YOU ARE NOT YOUR SCORE}

We are designed to seek definition, to seek category, to seek order from chaos. Electrical impulses pour into our brains from each of our five senses (sight, touch, taste, sound and smell). Our brains have a very sophisticated system – using the electrical input to form thoughts and act upon them accordingly – to make order of this flood of incoming information.

As we navigate life, it simply makes sense for us to try to group each other too – trying to make sense of the differences, of the nuances, that we each feel in ourselves and see in others. The problem is that as we seek to label and systematically define each other, there is no single test that can define an entire being.

The slice of information measured in any test is so very thin compared to the entirety of who each one of us truly is and who each one of us was created to be. Your gift is your unique piece of infinity and eternity.

It is humbling trying to explain eternity with science, because science provides only a rudimentary explanation of an infinite concept. Consider the fact that God said that His thoughts are above our thoughts (Isaiah 55:9), that we are "made in His own image" (Genesis 1:26-27) and that "we have the mind of Christ" (1 Corinthians 2:16), meaning He has given each of us just a small glimpse of His thinking!

Imagine this: God is eternity and infinity. He gifted each of us with a unique piece of His thinking to achieve a unique purpose He designed us to fulfill. We are more than equipped to deal with life successfully. We have truth-value.

Often, when we are grouped into boxes – learning disabled, gifted, right brained, left brained, overachiever, underachiever or any other box which seems to fit nicely at the time – that definition becomes a part of how we see ourselves.

However, you are so much more than what any label can define you as.

The IQ movement has led us to believe that we are either gifted or not gifted, that you have a high IQ or a low IQ, that you can or can't go to a university, that you are below average or average or brilliant. These IQ tests and other labels evaluate us at a fairly young age and can follow us the rest of our lives. In fact, many people have been incorrectly led to believe that intelligence is determined between ages 5 and 7, and thereafter nothing can change it.

Thankfully, we are living in a revolutionary time. Using the latest research, we can now clearly prove that intelligence is not fixed but rather grows and develops with us as we use it. Just like your gift.

You've had it inside of you all along, but it only grows and develops if you uncover it and use it properly.

Wherever you are in your education, your career or your life – with all the responsibilities you've been given – you can grow and develop into who you were truly created to be.

There is not an expiration date on potential.

We can see this clearly in science too, as we understand more now than ever before about the neuroplasticity of the brain – the ability the brain has to rewire itself.[1] This proves that the networks in our brains can change. If the brain gets damaged, it can change to compensate, proving that God is serious in Scripture when He tells us to renew our minds (Romans 12:2). Renewing our minds is a physical reality and scientific fact!

If we work with how our brains are wired, we can develop and change areas of our brains and live out our true selves. That's why the Gift Profile in Part Two measures the structure of your gift. When you know how your gift is structured, how your brain is uniquely wired, and how to achieve lasting success, you will unlock your truth-value – your gift.[2]

Unlike many conventional tests, the Gift Profile is a way to measure the structure of your gift, your strengths, instead of weaknesses. When you know your strengths and begin using them to receive information, your brain achieves efficiency and your non-dominant areas actually become stronger, because you are no longer relying on your brain to compensate for receiving information that doesn't work with how it's built.

In fact, you don't even have weaker areas; some are just non-dominant. This unique combination of dominance and non-dominance (I will explain this in later chapters) makes you special.

In Our Differences, We Find Greatness
Up to the mid-twentieth century, much of our knowledge about the brain was a mixture of speculation and dogmatism.

Now with the advances in brain imaging techniques over the last thirty years, we are getting a view of the brain operating in real time. The operating principle of brain imaging is that the more the activity in the brain – the more blood will flow to that area, supplying the oxygen and glucose to the hardworking neurons.[3]

From these imaging studies, along with other magnificent research by enlightened men and women in the field of brain research (see my reading list for some of this incredible research), we now know that the brain never wears out and that, in fact, it gets better with use. That's because more connections are made, creating more context and a depth of knowledge to draw upon. What's more, it changes its structure and function throughout our lives, adding to the uniqueness of how wonderfully we are made. We quite literally shape our own brains according to the choices we make – I call this the "I-factor" – and our life experiences.

The exciting result of this plasticity of the brain that we hold power over is that no two brains are alike: We are uniquely, fearfully and wonderfully made (Psalm 139:14). There is diversity in brain structure and organization and function, which results in the way we think and approach life.

And as we carry this thought over into the classroom, I believe that sometimes what is diagnosed as a learning disability is actually classroom induced. Not all children are wired to sit still and absorb information. When we don't work with the structure of our gifting, our ability to process information and build memory can be blocked.[4]

For example, after we discover that a child labeled with learning disabilities has a kinesthetic gift structure – the dominant way information enters his brain is closely linked with movement – we can then think about strategies to maximize opportunities for him to learn by working with how his brain is wired.

In some circumstances, children who are kinesthetic are given a ball to sit on, rather than a stationary chair. You may have seen these balls in the gym or in ergonomically-designed offices. You can even get a little ball for a seat, so that the child can rock from side to side, which is easy to carry from classroom to classroom. Interestingly, the side-to-side movement actually allows information to enter the brain in the sequence used in the child's brain wiring. It might be unconventional, and in a context that is not balanced it could even be distracting. But for that child, a simple chair swap could be revolutionary.

But this wouldn't work with everyone. If you are not a dominant kinesthetic, it wouldn't help at all. In fact, it would probably only cause you frustration.

How you operate, learn and process and what you do with your gift are all going to be different for you than for anyone else, according to the measurable structure of your gift. Understanding this will give you the freedom to work within whatever system you are in – at a school, an office or your home – to achieve the balance that you need to grow in your gift.[5]

Although you may be long out of elementary school, the principle of swapping out your chair for a metaphorical bouncing ball applies to you too. I have even had a CEO of a major corporation swap out his office chair for a ball!

When you understand how your brain is wired, how you were designed to move through the world, how your gift is structured, you can unlock your true self, your God-ordained self. You can learn more quickly, think more clearly, process faster, accomplish more and become a better leader when you see other people for how they are uniquely wired.

The purpose of your gift is to celebrate your difference, not minimize or squash it so that you can live in uniformity with everyone else around you. It is in our differences that we find greatness and can glorify our Creator.

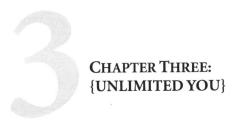

CHAPTER THREE:
{UNLIMITED YOU}

> " . . . you knit me together in my mother's womb. I praise you
> because I'm fearfully and wonderfully made . . . "
> (Psalm 139:13-14 NIV).

You were created intentionally. You have been knit together in a particular way. Nothing about you is a surprise to God. He knows you inside and out, and He did not design you to be limited.

When I first started to study the science of thought, how we think and how we process, I was overwhelmed by what my research uncovered. Over and over, I saw Scripture proven in the scientific principles being discovered by giants in the field of neuroscience. My commitment has always been to seek out how my research has its genealogy in the Word of God.

Conventional wisdom for years held that the brain doesn't grow or change after early childhood and, as we age, that our brain progressively degenerates and lets us down. Also, it was believed that once the brain was damaged it would always be damaged.[6]

However, the newly-emergent science of neuroplasticity shows that the brain has the ability to reorganize itself, changing and altering its structure as we think. The brain can adjust to trauma and rewire toxic thoughts and learning patterns. This has profound implications that can break the chains of the past – the brain can grow and change as we think, all under our control. Neuroplasticity research is outlining the boundless potential of the human brain and providing hope, a far cry from the theory of the unchanging brain.[7]

When I started my research, neurologists told me I was wasting my time trying to improve the mental activity of a traumatically brain-injured patient. Well, I am happy to say that by working with how the brain was designed to function and through hard work, lasting change was achieved.[8]

It's incredibly exciting to realize that what we choose to think about and how we choose to think can switch our genes on and off, changing the structure and function of the brain. The way in which we think will impact the health of our brains and our bodies.[9] The choices we make are governed by our thoughts, and we have full control over our thought lives. Even more exciting is the fact that we each have a unique and distinct gift that impacts *how we think.*

As we use our gifts, we are altering our brain anatomy. Although the basic brain structures are the same for all of us, the connections between the nerve cells are constantly changing each time we think and re-experience something. This means the connective architecture of the brain differs dramatically between people because of *how we think,* the structure of our gifts.

Furthermore, the more We think, the more connections we grow, making the memory storage area of the brain thicker and causing us to become more intelligent.[10] The more intelligent we become, the deeper we think, and the more our gifts grow.

But here's the catch: we can alter brain anatomy in a positive love direction or a negative fear direction by how and what we choose to think, choices we make and succeeding actions, behaviors and words we speak. It's entirely up to us.[11]

If we start building fear pathways by entertaining toxic thinking, such as bitterness, worry, anxiety, anger, unforgiveness and so on, we can wire negative and rigid behaviors into the brain, which become "gift-blockers."

The phenomenal plasticity of the brain makes it creative but also susceptible to gift-blockers. Scientists call this the "plastic paradox" of the brain, meaning an amazing characteristic is used for the wrong purpose, harming instead of healing.

When you think, you change your brain. When you think according to your own unique sequence, walking in your gift, you change the brain in an ever-positive direction. By understanding the impact of healthy non-toxic thinking and unhealthy toxic thinking on your gift, you can truly begin to understand the extent of the possibilities our Creator has placed within us.

Another fascinating thing about the brain's incredible ability to change is that there cannot be plasticity in isolation, meaning that if one brain system or an element of the structure of your gift changes, then the systems connected with it will change as well.[12] This is exciting because it means that positive change in one area of your brain will lead to positive change in other areas as well.

Of course we have to remember the converse is also true. Gift-blockers affect all the areas around them, literally spreading the negative message and increasing toxicity. A gift-blocker has a damaging chemical and physical effect on the brain, resulting in inflammation, which interrupts the cycle of thought in some way and hinders your ability to think clearly.

You have a divinely pre-wired gift to achieve a unique and divine purpose. In Part Two, as you uncover your gift, you will uncover your purpose, potential and provision, allowing you to tear down any gift-blockers in your way.

*But whoever did want him, who believed he was who he claimed and would do what he said, He made to be **their true selves, their child-of-God selves** (John 1:9 The Message).*

Discovering Your Truth-Value

There is a spiritual principle that underlies the release of your truth-value, your talent, your gift. If you use what God has given to you, you will grow into who He created you to be – your God self (Psalm 82:6, John 10:34-36). In the science of thought, this God self, this piece of eternity – your truth-value – is the way you think, the pattern of your thoughts, which is distinct and special to you.

Your gift lies in something so profound yet so simple that we tend to overlook it: the combination of your life experiences with the measurable structure of how your brain has been wired to think and process information.

God's thoughts are higher than your thoughts, but He has given you a piece of His thoughts by equipping you to think in the distinct way you think. Einstein once said, "I want to know God's thoughts . . . the rest are details." This is one of my favorite quotes, because it so aptly captures what the gift in us really is. And now, do you still wonder about the battles that rage in our thought lives? The enemy will use any gift-blocker he can get his hands on to mess up your thought life and disconnect you from your Savior.

We have a responsibility to steward the gift despite all the gift-blockers (circumstances, thoughts) that get in our way. In Scripture, I believe the parable of the talents (Matthew 25:14-30) demonstrates how we are called to be good stewards of more than just our finances or opportunities; God has also called us to steward our minds, our bodies, our potential and above all, our gifts which allow us to perform all of the above.

Only when you voluntarily surrender your whole self to God can you release that truth-value, your gift, your piece of eternity. It isn't the reason to surrender, but it is one of the blessings of surrendering your life to Christ.

Because each of us has a unique gift, we each walk in our gifting differently. You can't compare your gift to anyone else's, and when you walk in your own gift a few things will follow. Love is one, wisdom another.

Chapter Four:
{Operating in Your Gift}

Operating in your gift allows you to choose love and not fear. God has hardwired your gift. We all seek for others to understand us, but what most of us don't realize is that no one else can understand us until we understand who we are created to be.

When you find a problem you can uniquely solve, when you understand your gift and its structure and operate in it, you then find your truth-value, who you were created to be. You move beyond yourself into serving others. You will find peace in the image you were likened after. You will find peace in belonging and begin making a difference as one of the created pieces of the puzzle.

When you are truly fulfilled and at peace, when you know who you are in Christ, He can use you to help others find their fit in the puzzle. This is love.

Deep inside us is the awareness of self, the awareness of our higher calling, and the desire to be understood. Our cry as we go through life is, "Does anyone out there understand me?" When we operate out of fear of rejection, fear of pain and fear of abuse, we cannot believe anyone wants to understand us; our fears work to thwart the desire for love and acceptance God hardwired inside of each of us.

Science has shown that fear rewires our brains in a negative direction, destroying our truth-value and blocking our gifts. This leads to toxic thoughts, toxic attitudes and toxic lives.[13]

Too often we seek an answer in other places when we should be looking to our creator. He created you as a thinking being – the science of thought shows us the material evidence of this fact. Expanding on the science of thought is the magnificence of the gift knitted into you, the gift that sets you apart for a special work. God said, "I knew you before I formed you in your mother's womb. Before you were born I set you apart . . ." (Jeremiah 1:5 NLT). Spiritually and scientifically, you were no accident of fate. You were specifically designed and created with love and in love to express love. Your gift operates within love.

Your thinking pattern is so powerful that it changes your genetic expression constantly and restructures your brain.[14] You are the <u>only</u> one who has control over this, and you wield this through the choices that you make.

So, you are an exclusive "designer brand," one of a kind.[15] Inside every cell in your body is your full makeup of DNA. Studies of twins show us that even though they have identical DNA, they are different because they think differently. Their unique way of thinking changes their genetic expression.[16]

Wisdom has built a house; she has carved its seven columns. She has prepared a great banquet, mixed the wines, and set the table. She has sent her servants to invite everyone to come. She calls out from the heights overlooking the city. "Come in with me," she urges the simple. To those who lack good judgment, she says, "Come, eat my food, and drink the wine that I have mixed. Leave your simple ways behind, and begin to live; learn to use good judgment" (Proverbs 9:1-6 NLT).

When You Operate in Your Gift, You Operate in Wisdom
Proverbs 9:1-6 likens wisdom to building a house on seven columns, preparing a banquet, taking part in the banquet, and using the house.

The implications are that wisdom and good judgment are built and take time to develop. Throughout the Word of God, we are instructed to get wisdom. It's not a choice. It's an instruction to build a house of wisdom in our minds.

Scientifically, the brain is also built on Seven Pillars, which, when used properly, produce clear, intelligent and wise thinking.[17] These seven main areas of the brain were revealed through imaging techniques that observe activity in people's brains as they perform different tasks.

We will discuss these Seven Pillars more, but it is important that God's Word and His wisdom are the strongest foundation. Brain science is very clear on the benefits of thinking deeply to develop the brain's intelligence and wisdom. As a popular phrase in the world of neuro-science puts it, "Use it or lose it." The more you think, the more your brain grows, making you wiser and more intelligent.

The development of your brain is under your own control. We are not victims of biology or environment. Our brains were designed with an ability to restructure and rewire, to control our reactions to circum-stances and events in our lives, and to develop our wisdom.

You perceive the world in the creative brilliance of your mind through seven types of thought.

Although you are not handed a roadmap for your life, there are road markers to ensure you are walking in your gifting – love and wisdom.

It may have been a while since you last spent time thinking about your brain – not your mind, your actual brain. You may have even struggled with that in classes but despite your past experience with the science of thought, it is important you understand how the brain works so you can understand how *your* brain works.

5

CHAPTER FIVE:
{THE SCIENCE OF YOUR GIFT}

Your brain is made of nerve cells, a hundred billion more or less, and each cell looks like a tree with a central cell body and branches.[18] Every thought makes up one of these nerve cells, with memories and other information growing off of it – the branches of the tree. For every "thought tree" you have in the left side of your brain, you have a duplicate, a mirror image, in the right side.[17]

God's design of how we store information is so inspiring. On the left side of your brain you draw on details to form the big picture, while on the right you draw from the big picture to find the details. So the same information is processed in two different ways, on both sides of your brain.

That means, in order to understand something and build a stable memory that augments intelligence, the two mirror images of the same "thought tree" have to communicate with one another. The right side of the brain must communicate with the left side of the brain; both sides of the brain must work in harmony, or in synergy, with each other, which means God designed you and your brain for intellectual depth. The more branches you grow on these nerve cells and the more they communicate with each other, the more intelligent you become.[19]

Neuron Forest

Golgi stain of the "magic trees" of the mind

Designed and created by Dr. Caroline Leaf
and Dr. Peter Amua-Quarshie
Illustrated by Green Grass Studios, LLC

When you operate in your gifting, these branches are able to form more easily, because your brain is working the way it was wired to support your gift. The way you process information, the way you problem solve, the way you use your unique insight – these are integral components to your gift and cannot be separated. (We will discover the structure of your gift in Part Two.)

Einstein is one of my favorite examples of someone who harnessed the ability of his gift, developed his gifting, and worked with how his brain was wired to benefit us all with the great advances he achieved.[20]

As you may already know, Einstein only learned to speak at three years of age, yet he was one of the greatest scientific minds in history. In 1905, Einstein's "miracle year," he revolutionized the concepts of physics and electromagnetism, and his equation e=mc2 is probably the most well known in the world. He made headlines all his life, even after his death in 1955.[21]

Although Einstein encouraged others to pursue their unique gifts during his lifetime, interestingly, we have also learned a great deal from his death about how each one of us is gifted. In a morbid detail, the doctor who performed Einstein's autopsy, Dr. Thomas Harvey of Princeton Hospital, stole his brain.[22]

Can you imagine? He sectioned Einstein's brain and preserved it. Believing it would reveal the secrets of genius, he never gave up on this belief his whole life. He sent slivers of the brain to doctors and scientists around the world who he believed would help in this endeavor. Eventually, he donated the brain back to science to be examined and studied. Einstein's brain now resides at Princeton Hospital under the watchful eye of Dr. Elliot Krauss.

What began then, and is still continuing now, is this search for the mystery of genius. As you can imagine, some interesting discoveries were made. In 1985, Dr. Marion Diamond at UCLA found that Einstein's brain had a higher ratio of glial cells to neural cells. Considering a glial cell supports and provides nutrition and housekeeping for the neurons in the brain, the theory goes that the more glial cells there are, the more thinking activity has been going on and the harder the brain has been working. She specifically noted that there were a larger amount of glial cells in the left parietal cortex (top sides of the brain that process sensory information, spatial orientation, logic, mathematical ability, spatial reasoning and three-dimensional visualization).[23]

Then in 1996, Dr. Sandra Witelson at MacMaster University in Ontario studied a few sections that Harvey gave her and discovered that Einstein did indeed have a larger parietal lobe and that the neurons were packed closely together, enabling them to communicate faster than normal, which may have contributed to Einstein's quick and extremely integrated thinking.[24]

At this point, even with all the incredible discoveries about the brain, scientists don't know enough about the brain to ascertain with 100% accuracy what these findings mean, but Witelson's work is the going theory at the moment.

One idea was that the brain was compensating because Einstein was slightly learning disabled. However, with the understanding of the science of gifting, it is easy to see that these areas of his brain were so developed, not because Einstein was learning disabled, but because those were the areas of his gifting, areas which he had developed greatly with his work and discoveries. These areas of his brain he had developed with purpose.

Although Einstein never took the Gift Profile, it is interesting to apply its underlying principle to understand the structure of his gift. Of course, using someone we are all familiar with is simply an illustration of how understanding the structure of our gifts can help us understand how best to walk in our gifts. However, this is simply a hypothesis based on historical research and is not Einstein's actual Gift Profile.

Einstein used his brain and his unique and remarkable way of thinking extensively. He thought hard and deeply according to his gift.[25] Einstein's own words describing his thought processes are fascinating: "Words do not play any roles. There are more or less clear images."[26]

This introspection regarding his scientific thought processing reveals a thing or two: To kick start his thinking process at the deepest level, logical, mathematical ability, spatial reasoning and three-dimensional visualization housed in the areas of his parietal lobe and occipital lobe (at the back of the brain) were engaged. These are also the areas where significant changes have been noticed in the study of Einstein's brain.

So rather than sitting in a classroom taking notes, this probably means he initiated his deepest thinking using his logic and visual/spatial skills. This makes sense considering he discovered the theory of relativity by imagining riding on a light beam through space, seeing the ideas he was formulating in pictures and then capturing these images in mathematical equations and words.[27]

But we will explore this in more depth in Part Two.

Let's just begin to realize at this point that genius is in all of us when we use our gifts. And as we use our gifts, physical change happens in the brain because of its neuroplasticity, which will be physically evidenced on a structural and chemical level in the brain. We don't have to find the genius factor in Einstein's brain and then try to assimilate this into our own brains.

Instead of trying to find the key to genius and intellect in the folds of Einstein's brain, we should rather glean from all this research that when he used it according to his gifting, he developed genius and changed the world. He solved a problem . . . a few in fact.

You can do the same. We would make lousy Einsteins, but we are great as ourselves.

Find your own gift.

Let's have a look at how we can begin to do this. Each one of us has Seven Pillars of thought – the foundation that launches our unique gifts.

Each one of us also has two primary areas of our brains where thoughts and memories are built. They are our top two pillars in the Gift Profile, which uncovers the structure of our gifts. Those are the areas through which you receive and build your temporary memories.

We can guess from the research that Einstein's top two strengths in the structure of his gift were Logical/Mathematical and Visual/Spatial. That explains why the connections in these two areas of his brain were so profoundly dense. After reviewing his life, it is easy to identify how he operated within his gifting.

This is just one illustration of how someone used his gifting to such great extent; everyone has the potential to do amazing things. Everyone is created to do something no one else can, and understanding the structure of our gifts allows us to discover and achieve that purpose.

Let's start by looking at these Seven Pillars and your Gift Profile.

PART TWO: Uncovering the Gift in You

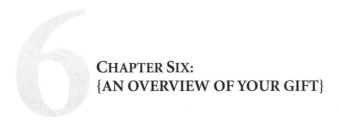

CHAPTER SIX:
{AN OVERVIEW OF YOUR GIFT}

Understanding the structure of your gift will help you learn how to maximize it, how you can work to achieve lasting results in any environment and how you can better relate to others who have their own unique gifts.

Sometimes, one of the greatest challenges can be interacting with people who think differently than you do. This can create challenges in both understanding what the other person is trying to communicate and in communicating with the other person.

But when we understand the structure of our own gifts and recognize the gifting of others, we have an opportunity to maximize any situation.

For example, I'm often asked to help business leaders develop their gifting further. One of the most interesting moments I've had was in the middle of a problem-solving activity at a company. It became very obvious that the company had little understanding or grace for each others' differences. This particular company was also experiencing a time of great stress. I quickly understood the problems the company was facing in business could very well have been rooted in the problems the employees were having with one another.

On one side of their huge conference table sat a guy who was about six-foot-eight and looked like he could play professional football – he was just missing the football gear. He had an obvious dislike for his colleague who was sitting directly across the table from him who happened to be around my height. Since I'm five-foot-two, there was an obvious physical disadvantage between the two men.

As we were working through problem solving, the tension just kept increasing and increasing. Finally, the tallest of the pair climbed on the table and was about to literally pick up his counterpart by the collar – apparently, he'd had enough. As he was reaching down, I realized in order to avert a brawl, it might be wise to use that moment as an illustration of how important it is to understand how we are wired differently. Either that or we all needed to duck for cover.

So, before he moved any further, I asked that they take a look at both of their Gift Profiles to see what their dominant pillars were. Turns out, they were polar opposites. The one standing on the table was Kinesthetic and Visual/Spatial, communicating what he saw in his mind's eye through action. His counterpart, on the other hand, was Logical/Mathematical and Linguistic.

The smaller gentleman was always trying to speak persuasively, but he was just speaking the big gentleman across the table into an absolute frenzy. Once I had showed them the differences in the structure of their gifts and how to better understand each other, the lightbulbs switched on, and by the end of the training session they walked out as better friends.

The Structure of Your Gift

As we reviewed in Part One, Proverbs 9:1 talks about wisdom being built on Seven Pillars. Here's the exciting part – just as the sequence of processing a thought isn't exactly the same for each one of us, the area of the brain stimulated to handle each one of the seven steps is different.

We have been taught that each section of the brain is responsible for specific functions. But the truth is the brain is sophisticated beyond measure; there are revolutionary discoveries about the brain being made as modern technology advances, allowing us to take a more comprehensive look at the brain than ever before. As we have gained more knowledge through imaging technology of the inside of the brain, areas of function in the brain are becoming more clearly defined.

From this science, we can see that the brain has seven main areas, which are like columns or pillars. Sound familiar? A house of wisdom, according to Scripture, is built on Seven Pillars, and according to science, the structure of your gift is also built on Seven Pillars.

So, what exactly are these pillars of thinking in the brain? The brain is made up of about a hundred billion nerve cells – which look a lot like trees and what I like to call "thought trees" – in your brain, pretty incredible when you consider your brain is only about the size of your two fists.

These thought trees group together forming Seven Pillars that run roughly from the top to the bottom of the brain across the left and right sides of the brain, and each one is responsible for a specific type of behavioral function, a specific type of thought. And although we cannot precisely explain how the actions of the nerve cells lead to a type of thought, we can estimate this from all the brain research that has been done over the years.

Although there are seven basic types of thought proposed, we must realize that there are an infinite number of descriptions of each type of thought and that all seven types work together, not in isolation, to create the true you. So you can't describe yourself as Visual or Logical and so on: You are a mixture of all seven types of thought making up your special way of perceiving the world.[1]

The combination of how these pillars of thinking of the brain work together and process information is what makes you, well, the true you. Because all humans have more or less the same areas that perform the similar functions, your differences (how these interact and change as you use them) are what make you special.[2]

All your thoughts/memories and emotions that make up you are stored in the non-conscious part of your mind and have a tremendous influence on your conscious thoughts. In fact our conscious mind is completely controlled by our non-conscious mind.[3]

If we have a toxic thought activated in the nonconscious and it's brought into consciousness, then your conscious thinking becomes toxic. Scientists have found that the nonconscious mind performs around 400 billion actions per second and the conscious mind is only aware of 2000 bits of information. So there is an enormous amount of exceptionally high-speed things going on in our minds as we think through our gift processing information.[4]

The depth of processing in these Seven Pillars of thinking is combined and used differently in every single person, which means that there are as many combinations as there are people, and consequently that traditional IQ and personality tests are limited and definitely do not define you or your future. You are an original!

You can take every single "type A" personality on the planet and you will discover that each one of them has a different combination of the Seven Pillars of thinking – each person is more than a label or a limited test. It is our differences that make us who we are. And it is in our differences that our gifts and resultant genius lie.

As neurons fire, for example, in the Linguistic area of your brain, they are activated to deal with sounds, perception, language and associative memories, because this is what the neurons in the temporal lobe area are specialized to do.

So, the neurons in the front of the brain – the frontal cortex that is the location of the **Intrapersonal pillar** – deal with decision-making, planning, deep-analyzing, shifting between thoughts, realizing goals and developing strategies. When we are introspective, we are using this type of thought.

Just behind the Intrapersonal pillar is the **Interpersonal pillar**, which is involved in social interaction, communications, turn-taking and tuning into the needs of others.

The Intrapersonal pillar is followed by the **Linguistic pillar**, which deals with spoken and written language.

After the Linguistic pillar is the **Logical/Mathematical pillar,** which deals with reasoning, logic, scientific thinking, numbers and problem solving.

Next is the **Kinesthetic pillar** that provides sensory and body awareness.

Then comes the **Musical pillar**, which of course is music-based, but also includes the ability to read between the lines and distinguish "gut instincts."

Finally, there is the **Visual/Spatial pillar** at the back of the brain, which is where we imagine and form mental maps.

Your unique thinking pattern requires that you think by moving through the seven different pillars of the brain's thought in a particular order, with a signature amount of bandwidth given to that function (which is signified, as an estimate, by your scores in the Gift Profile).

The Seven Pillars of Thinking

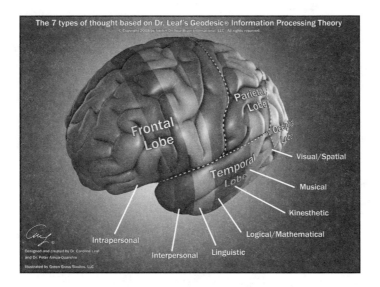

The 7 types of thought based on Dr. Leaf's Geodesic® Information Processing Theory

© Copyright 2008 by Switch On Your Brain International, LLC. All rights reserved.

Parietal Lobe

Frontal Lobe

Occipital Lobe

Temporal Lobe

Visual/Spatial

Musical

Kinesthetic

Logical/Mathematical

Intrapersonal

Interpersonal

Linguistic

Designed and created by Dr. Caroline Leaf
and Dr. Peter Amua-Quarshie

Illustrated by Green Grass Studios, LLC

Because each of us needs every pillar in order to function, each one of us has a sequence of thought that includes each pillar. We go through this each time we think and process information in a looping fashion.

As you operate in your gift, each thought loops through these Seven Pillars to develop the information into a picture of meaning, much like a photo is developed from a negative. The electrical information your five senses are gathering becomes a part of you — triggering memories, thoughts and actions.

The structure of how you develop information through this looping through the Seven Pillars creates your unique perception of the world, giving it your own special meaning, your own flavor. Each time you loop through these seven types of thought to create meaning, this immaterial mind activity leaves material traces. So, as you think and imagine, every thought alters the physical state of your brain synapses at a microscopic level. Each time you think using your gift, your brain changes.

When information loops through the Seven Pillars, the sequence of which is determined by your gift, a thought develops properly.

You can discover the structure of your gift. This will help you understand the nature of our own unique gift and how to develop it.

The mind is what the brain does, and we see the uniqueness of each mind through our gifts. This in itself is delightful and, intriguing because, as you work out your gift and find out who you are, you will be developing your soul and spirit. After all, the Bible says: "Beloved, I pray that you may prosper in all things and be in health, just as your soul prospers" (3 John 1: 2 NKJV).

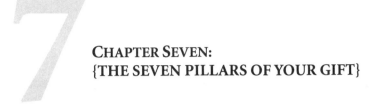

CHAPTER SEVEN:
{THE SEVEN PILLARS OF YOUR GIFT}

Each of the types of thought has its own developmental sequence, emerging and blossoming at different stages over a lifetime. "Humanness" comes from the interaction of all of these.[5]

As I mentioned earlier, there are an infinite number of sub-skills within each of these pillars of thinking, and I want you to be able to apply the Gift Profile and the structure of your gift to you – wherever you may be. This book is an overview, using very broad definitions. If you are interested in the scientific nuance, I've included a list of Recommended Reading in Appendix A. I encourage you to use this Recommended Reading list to dive into the science of the brain further.

When we start exploring the Seven Pillars of thought, an integral principle is that all seven of these pillars work together very, very intimately. They don't work separately, and they are all interconnected.

Another principle is that, as a human being, you have a sequence of these types of thought, which can be identified from highest to lowest. So when you complete the Gift Profile, you can actually see the structure of your gift and the order of the different types of thinking.

It is important to note that the Gift Profile is not like a standardized test. A "better" score is not a "high" score in each area. In fact, it is impossible for all areas of the Gift Profile to have a high score.

It's impossible, because God didn't design you to have all of them equally or for you to be the same as everyone else – we are not robots.

This is the gifting principle: We do not all have the same gift.

What Is the Function of a Pillar?

Each of the Seven Pillars of thinking is responsible for primary functions and particular characteristics. Accordingly, it is always interesting to learn about each function (see image on page 46).

Let's start at the front of the brain and move to the back, but remember, this is not necessarily the sequence of how your gift is structured. Your brain may process a thought in a different sequence. This is simply a deeper look at what each pillar of thought making up your gifting is to help you understand more clearly.

Intrapersonal Intelligence

At the front of the brain we have our Intrapersonal pillar, our intrapersonal level of thought. All the nerve cells in this area are basically tuned to handle information that deals with deep-thinking, decision-making, pulling things together, focusing, analyzing and free will.

Intrapersonal thinking is at the heart of you standing outside of yourself and looking in to analyze your own thinking. This is where the seat of free will comes into play as, while we analyze incoming and existing information, we are going to make decisions about what to think, say and do.

This pillar is fundamental to introspection, self-knowledge and understanding your own feelings, thoughts and intuitions. The ability to access these allows you to guide your behavior, understand your strengths and weaknesses, imagine concepts, plan activities and solve problems. This pillar also incorporates self-discipline.

If Intrapersonal intelligence is your dominant pillar (the first pillar in your thought sequence), then you receive information best through introspection and reflection. This is like the doorway into your thinking processing – the way to kick start the process.

If Intrapersonal thinking is near the top of your thinking pattern, you may display a few or all of these qualities:

- You are introspective and aware of your range of emotions.
- You have the ability to control and work with your thoughts and emotions.
- You find ways of expressing your thoughts.
- You are motivated to identify and pursue goals.
- You work well independently.
- You are curious about the meaning of life.
- You self-manage ongoing personal learning and growth.
- You attempt to understand inner experiences.
- You empower and encourage others.
- You like solitude and are happy to work alone.
- You enjoy thinking strategies, journal writing, relaxing and self-assessment strategies.
- You understand your limitations.
- You have the ability to assess and evaluate situations.

Here is a short list of possible professions that people with high Intrapersonal thinking often gravitate to:

- Judge
- Counselor
- Advocate

- Educator
- Lawyer
- Therapist
- Novelist
- Psychiatrist
- Philosopher
- Elder
- Mathematician
- Visionary Leader

Interpersonal Thinking

Just behind the Intrapersonal thinking area is the Interpersonal thinking area. These nerve cells are all responsible for communicating – not simply talking but communicating.

Social interaction, listening, sharing, building relationships, giving and receiving love – these are all primary functions of this pillar. Interpersonal thinking gives us the ability to understand and work well with people.

This pillar incorporates sensitivity to and empathy with others, particularly for their moods, desires, motivations, feelings and experiences. It allows us the ability to respond appropriately to others as well. This pillar involves the ability to "read" other people's moods, to "put oneself in another person's shoes." It enables you to pick up inconsistencies when listening to smooth talkers so you know who to trust.

It also refers to good managerial and mediating skills, and the ability to motivate, lead, guide and counsel others.

If the Interpersonal pillar is near the top of your thinking pattern you may display a few or all of these qualities:

- You are a strong leader.
- You are good at networking.
- You can negotiate.
- You can teach.
- You enjoy bouncing ideas off other people.
- You love to talk.
- You like to organize.
- You happily mediate in disputes and are good at conflict resolution.
- You enjoy acting as a mentor to others.
- You have the ability to focus outward on other people.
- You sense other people's moods, temperaments, motivations and intentions.
- You have the ability to influence others.
- You excel at group work, team efforts and collaborative work.
- You bond with people.
- You form lasting social relationships.

Here is a short list of possible professions that people with high Interpersonal thinking gravitate to:

- Politician
- Religious Leader
- Salesperson
- Educator
- Counselor
- Social Worker
- Speech/Language Therapist
- Occupational Therapist
- Psychologist
- Public Relations Officer
- Human Resource Director
- Manager

Linguistic Thinking

Linguistic thinking is universal by nature and is present in all of us in varying degrees, as we all use it as a major means of communication. The Linguistic pillar deals with how effectively you are able to use language to express yourself. It also deals with your sensitivity to the meanings of words, sounds, rhythms and different uses of language.

If the Linguistic pillar is close to the top of your list in your gift sequence, words are important to you. This is expressed in different ways such as being articulate or having the ability to think in words and use words effectively when you speak and/or write. A dominant Linguistic pillar means that you primarily build memory through words – spoken, written, expressed or read.

You will have a natural leaning toward the domains that make up language, its structure and use. These include:

- Semantics: the meanings or connotations of words.
- Phonology: the sounds of words and their interactions with each other.
- Syntax: the rules governing the order in which words are used to create understandable sentences. One example is that a sentence must always have a verb.
- Pragmatics: how language can be used to communicate effectively.

If the Linguistic pillar is one of the first steps in the sequence of your gift, you may exhibit some of these characteristics:

- You need to express and explain yourself by writing and/or using lots of words.
- You like to argue, persuade, entertain and instruct.
- You like to write, play with words, read and tell stories.
- You have a good general knowledge.

- You ask a lot of questions.
- You like to lead and/or participate in discussions.
- You like storyboards, word processors and voice recorders.
- You love reading and need lots of books around you.
- You spell well.
- You learn languages easily.
- You have a good memory for names, dates and places.

Here is a short, and by no means all-inclusive list of possible professions that people with high Linguistic thinking gravitate to:

- Publicist
- Editor
- Speechwriter
- Poet
- Novelist
- Politician
- Copywriter
- Speech/Language Therapist
- Scriptwriter
- Lawyer/Attorney/Advocate
- Journalist
- Educator

Logical/Mathematical Thinking

The next pillar of thought is Logical/Mathematical, which deals with scientific reasoning, logic and analysis. This type of thinking involves your capacity to understand the underlying principles of a connecting system, recognize logical and numerical patterns, handle long chains of reasoning in a precise manner and manipulate numbers, quantities and operations.

This pillar also includes the ability to mentally calculate and process logical problems and equations, much like the types of problems most often found on multiple-choice, standardized tests.

If this is one of your primary pillars, then you have a natural leaning toward the domain of numbers and logic, including:

- Numbers: the ability to manipulate and use numbers effectively.
- Pattern Recognition: the ability to see the category, organization and association in nature, numbers, words, stories and life.
- Identification: the attempt to find meaning in things.

If your Logical/Mathematical pillar is one of the strongest pillars in your sequence of thought, you build memory through reasoning. Some characteristics you show will include:

- You are intuitive and disciplined in your thinking.
- You like to calculate and quantify.
- You want to reason things out.
- You want to know what's coming up next.
- You love to roam in the realm of imaginary and irrational numbers.
- You find paradoxes challenging.
- You love to create theories of how things work.
- You like to work out and fully understand complex sequences.
- You need systematic proof of something before using it.
- You show the ability to recognize and then solve problems.

Here is a short list of possible professions that people with Logical/ Mathematical thinking tend to gravitate to:

- Scientist
- Medical Doctor
- Mathematician
- Project Manager
- Accountant
- Lecturer
- Engineer
- Researcher
- Computer Programmer
- Pathologist
- Banker
- Forensic Scientist
- Lawyer
- Detective
- Animal Tracker
- Business
- Computer Analyst

Kinesthetic Thinking

Kinesthetic intelligence is the intelligence of movement, somatic sensation and moving around. Your Kinesthetic pillar helps you play soccer, run around, sit in a chair without falling off of it or navigate your way down an aisle. This pillar includes integrating your sensations from inside your body as well.

By definition, this is a very tactile, energetic, multisensory type of thinking that involves the control of body movements, the ability to co-ordinate yourself and the capacity to handle objects and things around you skillfully.

These kinds of thinkers need to touch, feel and move things around. To understand and retain information, they have to maneuver or experience what they learn.

Kinesthetic thinking is undervalued in most academic environments, which place a higher value on problem-solving and Linguistic approaches. Kinesthetic learners are the "busy body" types, the ones who learn best by moving around, the ones educators usually label as "naughty," "disruptive," "hyperactive" or "just plain stupid." Kinesthetic learners, of course, are none of these things; it's just that sitting in a classroom situation where someone just talks at them is not at all the ideal learning environment for them.

When faced with such a learning environment, Kinesthetic learners often feel as if information "goes in one ear and out the other." The fact is, it almost literally does just that. If they can only hear information, Kinesthetic learners' brains do not process information in a form that can be stored effectively in their memory banks, because they must build memory through movement.

If Kinesthetic thinking is strong (near the top) you may display a few or all of these qualities:

- You have good coordination.
- You show a good sense of timing.
- You approach problems physically.
- You explore your environment through touch and movement.
- You like to fiddle with and do things.
- You often stretch.
- You like role-play and drama.
- You love to dance.
- You need to move when thinking.
- You enjoy exercise.
- You enjoy crafts and hobbies.
- You demonstrate balance, dexterity, grace and precision in physical tasks.
- You invent new approaches to physical skills.

Here is a short list of possible professions that people with high Kinesthetic thinking follow:

- Actor
- Athlete
- Dancer
- Inventor
- Jeweler
- Sculptor
- Artist
- Electrician
- Mechanic
- Surgeon
- Race Car Driver
- Choreographer
- Artisan
- Occupational Therapist
- Physical Therapist

Musical Thinking

Musical intelligence might seem like it's the ability to sing or play a musical instrument – that's obvious – but surprisingly, it's also the ability to read patterns, identify rhythm, deal with instincts and, most importantly, *read between the lines.*

It works very extensively with the part of your brain called the insula, which is deep inside the Musical intelligence and helps you to actually have instinct, allowing you to read between the lines. It allows you to sense meaning and to verify it.

For example, when you ask your friend, "Are you okay?" and she says, "Yes, I'm fine" (with a quiver in her voice), this pillar allows you to actually read that she's not so fine.

It's the ability to read people, through their tone of voice and body language, rather than just listening to their words.

This Musical pillar incorporates sensitivity to pitch, melody, rhythm and tune in sounds and movements you hear and see around you, as well as the ability to produce rhythm, pitch and forms of musical expression.

It is also the intelligence of intuition, "gut-instinct" and reading body language. On one end of the human scale is the level of musical thinking attributed to interpretation of conversation, and on the other end of the scale is the level attributed to Mozart.

Some types of thought have a critical period for optimal development, and Musical intelligence is one of them. The years between the ages of four and six are the optimal time for developing sensitivity to sound and pitch. It is therefore during this time that musical ability is best developed. This does not mean, of course, that you will never be able to develop your ability beyond those years. All humans have the capacity to develop their Musical intelligence.

If this is a dominant pillar in your gift structure, then you build memory through rhythm and intuition.

However, no matter whether your Musical intelligence is high or low, music can still help you learn. Classical music, in particular, has proven to be beneficial in classrooms and other learning environments.

If your Musical intelligence is strong, then characteristics you may display include:

- You instinctively feel when things are right or wrong.
- You don't do things unless they "feel" right.
- You can't always explain why but you know when someone is to be trusted or not to be trusted.

- You are highly sensitive to your surroundings and feel comfortable or uncomfortable in certain places.
- You are able to "read between the lines" of what people are saying.
- You find yourself interpreting the meaning behind things.
- You seek out sound.
- You respond to music.
- You like to compose music.
- You play an instrument.
- You can sing in tune.
- You keep time to music.
- You instinctively listen critically to music.
- You listen and respond to environmental sounds.
- You collect songs, instruments and music.
- You create musical instruments.
- You use the vocabulary and notation of music.
- You hum often.
- You tend to tap your foot, finger or pen when working or listening.
- You offer interpretations of the meaning of music.
- You have a highly developed intuition.

Here is a short list of possible professions that people with high Musical thinking gravitate to:

- Conductor
- Instrument Maker
- Composer
- Mixing Engineer
- Piano Tuner
- Disc Jockey
- Music Educator
- Instrumentalist
- Performer

- Dancer
- Musician
- Singer
- Recording Engineer
- Public Speaker

Visual/Spatial Thinking

Visual/Spatial thinking is the ability to see color, light, shape and depth. You are able to close your eyes and imagine, seeing things that are not actually in front of your eyes.

Blind people have a very, very well developed Visual/Spatial intelligence, because they rely on what they see in their mind's eye.

Visual/Spatial intelligence is the ability to be able to see without seeing; for example, you can imagine a loved one and call up a visual image from your non-conscious into consciousness. This is the ability to visualize in pictures and/or images, to "see" with the mind's eye, to make mental maps, to perceive the visual/spatial world accurately, and to act on initial perceptions.

Visual/Spatial intelligence is about internally representing the spatial world out there in your mind and being able to orientate yourself in three-dimensional space with ease.

Artists have high Visual/Spatial thinking which expresses itself in great works of art like the masterpieces of Leonardo da Vinci and Michelangelo.

This type of thinking is not restricted to the arts. In Sir Isaac Newton and Albert Einstein, for example, the expression of their high Visual/Spatial thinking was more scientific. It also is not restricted to the physical sense of what something looks like.

If this type of thought is high up in your sequence, then you build memory through abstract language and imagery.

If your Visual/Spatial intelligence is high, some characteristics you show include:

- You often stare off into space while listening.
- You enjoy hands-on activities. That is, you learn by seeing and doing.
- You recognize faces but may not remember names.
- You navigate through spaces well; for example, you easily find your way through traffic.
- You think in pictures and visualize details easily.
- You perceive both obvious and subtle patterns and see things in different ways or from new angles. You are proficient in both representational and abstract design.

Here is a short list of possible professions that people with high Visual/Spatial intelligence gravitate to:

- Sculptor
- Archaeologist
- Leader
- CEO
- Graphic Designer
- Engineer
- Draftsperson
- Sailor
- Videographer
- Photographer
- Mathematical Topologist
- Painter
- Naturalist
- Navigator

- Battlefield Strategist
- Architect
- Pilot

Although you will have dominant pillars in the structure of your gift, you function using all seven. And it is our own unique sequence of our gift structures that forms how we process information, how we see the world.

For an example of the gift in action and how we all differ in such delightful ways, let me give you the "Persian Carpet" explanation.

Ulam Stanislow is a Nobel Prize-winning mathematician. As a young child, he was fascinated by the intricate patterns in Persian carpets. They seemed to produce a melody and a mathematical regularity to him. This demonstrates his strong Musical and Logical/ Mathematical thinking.

Someone with a different thinking sequence might have looked at the same carpet in a completely different way. For example, a person looks at the same rug and expresses it in poetic terms. That's the sign of a person whose Linguistic thinking is high.

Yet another looks at that same carpet and notices at once its placement in the room in relation to the furniture and color scheme. This person's Visual/Spatial thinking is high. A person with strong Interpersonal thinking might not notice the color of the carpet but focuses rather on the warmth and comfort it provides.

Finally, a person with strong Intrapersonal thinking might see the intricate patterns on the carpet as representing the intricacies of life – all the events from childhood to adulthood. We will all look at the rug differently and see different things because our perceptions are based on who we are, which, in turn, is determined by the unique sequence of the Seven Pillars that exist in each of us.

Now that you know a little about these seven different types of thinking, you can move on to working out your Gift Profile, which you will learn to do in the next chapter.

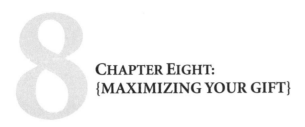

CHAPTER EIGHT:
{MAXIMIZING YOUR GIFT}

Understanding the structure of your gift is imperative to living out your gifting. Hosea 4:6 says: "My people are destroyed for lack of knowledge" (KJV). Let's not perish but rather soar as we move into a deeper understanding of our gifts and who we are.

You were wonderfully and beautifully made with specific intent and incredible purpose.

If you were meant to be the same as everyone else, everyone would have the exact same way of activating and expressing his or her genetic code. As I mentioned earlier, identical twins have the same genetic code, but the expression is different and is determined and influenced by the "I-factor" – our unique way of thinking. This is seen in how different twins are in their likes and dislikes and behavior and life choices and even in their susceptibility to disease. So twins have different experiences because of a factor, over and above the genes, that is called epigenetics. Epigenetics provides another scientific way of understanding how we are each so different. It tells us that externally-driven changes – like how we think and our reactions to the events of life – will influence the behavior of our genes.[6]

As we reviewed in Chapter 7, there are seven different areas of the brain stimulated (see page 46) when we process a thought, resulting in seven different types of thinking:

1. Intrapersonal – introspection
2. Interpersonal – interaction
3. Linguistic – words spoken and written

4. Logical/Mathematical – scientific and strategic reasoning, order, planning
5. Kinesthetic – movement, experiential
6. Musical – instinct, reading between the lines, musical talent
7. Visual/Spatial – imagination, seeing in the mind's eye

As we learned earlier, while all of us operate with all Seven Pillars of thought – the strength of each pillar is different for each one of us.

As we loop through the specific order of our gifts, the information goes through stages of processing. Like a photo has to be processed, our thoughts have to be developed into full-blown understanding or we won't use them properly.

It is good to process healthy thoughts using our gift, but when toxic thoughts are fully processed they can cause serious harm. Because they are negative they upset the electrical chemical balance in the brain because of the stress they cause. Along with a fixed structural change that now influences your thinking, they also bring a whole bunch of emotional and chemical toxic waste. This in turn starts hampering your gift in processing the good stuff, and the toxic thoughts will want to dominate and grow and influence your perceptions unless controlled. In Parts Three and Four we will explore this in more depth.

Let's first get a better understanding of how the gift develops:

- First, we receive the information from our five senses.
- Second, we build connections to this information from existing information and memories – helping our minds make sense of new information.

Inside the Brain

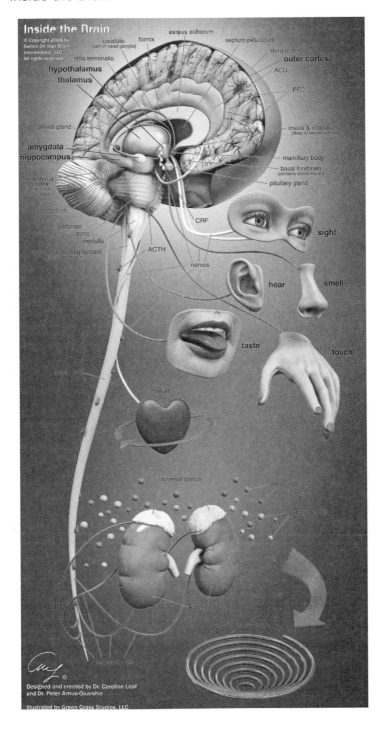

- Third, we consolidate this information in the "trees" (neural networks) in the cortex of our brains.
- Fourth, we confirm this information and decide if we feel it is true.
- Fifth, we integrate the information into the networks of the memories.
- Sixth, we apply the information to the present circumstance.
- Seventh, we close the open loop.

Until we move though these levels of processing, the thought won't be fully processed or have meaning. Obviously, this happens incredibly fast so you won't "feel" all these things happening; you will normally only be aware of the first two types of thought and perhaps the last one in your order (that you will determine from your Gift Profile coming up).

However, as you are looping through the Seven Pillars of thought in your particular order (your gift), you might start noticing how you "think through" information. This is a good thing to become aware of because it will help you identify when you have a gift-blocker in action. If there are any disruptions along this pathway in the form of gift-blockers, then you won't think it through properly. This in turn will affect your attitude and the decisions you make.

That's why uniqueness of consciousness, the fact that you are totally different from anyone else and can do what no one else can, is considered one of the most difficult things to explain – it's often termed the "hard question" in science.[7]

But if we take Proverbs 9 and principles from Scripture and pair them with ground-breaking brain science on which my "gift" theory is based, we can begin to explain this "hard question."

How does the order of the Seven Pillars of thought link to the processing of thought that is the same for each one of us?

Each step in the sequence of processing thought stimulates different areas of the brain – different pillars – in each one of us. The depth of stimulation in each area of the brain is also different for each of us.

For example, my dominant pillar is Interpersonal, and the first step in the sequence of thought (for everyone) is gathering information.

That means, if I were to be in a classroom, I would do best if I were gathering information while interacting with the teacher or the people around me. I would better process information if I asked questions, because it would jump start my brain's sequence of processing incoming information. Working on my own, I "ask" a lot of questions from books and research articles.

However, if your first pillar were Intrapersonal, you would most likely feel very frustrated if you were required to ask questions at this step in the process. This is because you would be listening deeply to receive the information you need to process and think through to understanding. Questions would interrupt this.

When we determine the structure of your gift – the order of the pillars that your brain uses to process information according to the proper sequence – we can determine triggers to maximize your brain function during every step.

Another important factor to consider when interpreting the results of the Gift Profile is how high the score is in each area. Remember, there isn't a "correct" score and no one score is better than another. In fact, the difference in each one of our scores is what is so amazing. This nuance is where each of our gifting lies – our strength is in our differences.

How high your score is for each of the pillars simply determines how profound that trait is in your gift and the order in which that loop works. If you have a really high score in one area, most likely those traits are very profound elements of your personality.

For example, if I were to score in the 70s on the Interpersonal Questionnaire, I most likely wouldn't need as much interaction during this step in the thinking sequence as I would need if my score were in the 90s.

If your first pillar were Intrapersonal and you scored in the 90s on the Intrapersonal Questionnaire, you most likely would need a lot of time at first to process information internally. If your score were in the 70s, you would need less time.

Perhaps the most important part of understanding the structure of your gift is *freedom*. When you understand, you will be free from any label – any label you've given yourself, any label the world has given you and, especially, any label you *think* the world has given you.

Unique Combinations

In my own family, I see every day how each one of our unique combinations really does have a powerful impact on how we function.

My husband Mac and I have four children. Although we all have common values and a lot of other things in common, it is our differences that add interest and adventure to how we work together as a family. When we reached the point of being able to recognize that our differences were our strengths, we were able to reach a level of peace and trust with one another – a level I don't think we would have otherwise been able to reach.

This is a reality for any family and any organization. The gift concept helps us to see each other through Jesus' eyes because otherwise we see everything from our own perspective and expect everyone to conform to our way of thinking.

I love to share examples about our children. Even if you don't have a spouse or children, as you move through these exercises, think about those you work with and anyone who is in your immediate support network and your friends – you'll be amazed at the revelation of why they do what they do. Remember: Its not just about you; it's about serving others.

Jessica

Our eldest daughter, Jessica, has Intrapersonal and Linguistic as her top two types of thinking, which means that the doorway into her soul is through thinking deeply and using words to build her temporary memories in the networks of her mind. Jessica is a very deep thinker, and as she has matured (she is now 18), she expresses herself through poetry and devours classic novels as her soul food.

She loves people, but needs lots of space to have alone time to introspect. Sometimes when her brothers and sisters invade her space too much she gets frustrated and in their words "bossy." She also loves order and cleanliness, which is largely a part of the third type of thinking in her order – Logical/Mathematical. She consolidates her thinking with logic and order.

Intrapersonal in the top position will often be the person who is the quietest in the group, the one reluctant to say much but who comes up with pearls of wisdom and deep insight when you least expect it.

Dominique

My second daughter, Dominique, has Visual/Spatial and Interpersonal as the top two in her order. An interesting pattern because Dominique's doorway into her mind consists of picturing what people are saying in her mind's eye and then asking loads of questions to build her temporary memory. She shifts between seeing, questioning, seeing, questioning and so on as she receives and builds the memory.

When Dominique was little and I spoke to her, she wouldn't look at me while I was speaking, and before I could finish, she would start asking questions. That was before my research on the gift was fully developed, and sometimes I would get quite frustrated because I thought that in order to really pay attention, eye contact was necessary. This is the thinking I had grown up with. But more than that, this is the way I begin to process – through eye contact and direct Interpersonal questioning. But this is not true and is actually an example of a perception being a gift-blocker, because someone who has Visual/Spatial in the top of his or her order sees things in his or her mind's eye, often making eye contact distracting as they receive the information. As she shifts to her second pillar to build the temporary memory, which in Dominique's case is Interpersonal thinking, she then begins to ask questions.

I'd always say, "Dominique, look at me and let me finish" – until I better understood the Seven Pillars and realized I should profile her. I'm so glad that I profiled my children early on. It really helped me understand who they are as individuals so we could understand who we are as a family.

After profiling Dominique and learning she had a very strong Visual/Spatial pillar, I understood why she doesn't look at me when I speak. She sees things in her mind's eye and mental map as she is being spoken to – that's how her brain processes. This enables Dominique to be very in control and think clearly in a crisis situation – she is a star at this because she "sees" solutions and communicates them, calming everyone.

In a classroom, Visual/Spatial children are often the ones looking down at their paper and drawing and doodling, even staring out the window while they listen. Visual/Spatial children might be very distracting to work with, until you realize that they are processing the information at the deepest level even when they don't make eye contact. When they look away, they are able to visualize in their heads what you're saying – looking away actually helps them build memory.

Recently I was working with a teacher in a school and midway through her lesson she commanded all the children to look at her and would not move on until they all did. I watched the class and noticed a couple of children look but their eyes glazed over, and I knew immediately they were looking but not seeing and were moving into their own mental maps to process what the teacher was about to say.

As you can see, when we can recognize these things, we can recognize how best to operate in our own gifts and how best to help others grow in theirs.

Jeffrey

My son Jeffrey has Logical/Mathematical and Visual/Spatial at the top of his thinking cycle. So, when he's playing or thinking, I know he's logically imagining in his mind. He comes up with the most incredible questions – firing them at the speed of light because the Linguistic type of thinking is his third pillar in the cycle and he expresses – often out loud – the thoughts he is logically visualizing. He consolidates memory and he builds thoughts through words. We can talk to him when he's ready to further process. I often catch myself trying to answer his questions as fast as he asks them and get frustrated in the process because he isn't really looking for the answer yet. I often made this mistake in the past. I would say things like, "Jeffrey, let me finish answering your question," and he would look at me all surprised because he hadn't even heard what I was saying. Once ready, he would then pause and look at me. Now I know that means, "I actually do now want an answer." We know that he is operating very deeply, so we allow him to have that space now, because we understand him.

Alexandria

I love describing my daughter Alexandria's gift, because so many people who have Kinesthetic at the top as their dominant pillar are misunderstood. If we had understood her gift earlier, we would also have had a much more peaceful household when she was young.

Out of the Seven Pillars, the dominant pillar for my youngest child Alexandria is Kinesthetic. When I try to teach her something or communicate with her, I always keep in mind that if there is any way to integrate movement or show her hands-on, she will learn better with something along those lines. If I just describe something to her with loads of words, I won't touch her soul or get through to who she really is and how she thinks. She may be able to repeat what I said, but for her to truly process it deeply there needs to be some hands-on learning, movement or "showing how" involved.

However, when she was very young – around 2 – her way of troubleshooting in any situation, or her approach to problem management was to use physical means to express her frustration. You know, if her brothers or sisters irritated her, she'd just kick whoever might be standing nearby.

Needless to say, as a parent, it was challenging.

Because she didn't have the verbal skills to reason at such a young age and because she's so Kinesthetic dominant, I now know that her process was something along the lines of, "I can't say it, so I'll just physically show you you're irritating me." As she got older and more verbal, we were able to teach her other ways to express herself.

Now Alexy is 11, so she's obviously older and can deal with issues really well. She is still physically expressive, which is apparent in her facial expressions. Now we can recognize when it's best to talk something out and when it's best to hit the deck. We'll say, "Oh, Alexy's having a Kinesthetic moment. Let's leave her alone." I have also found that giving her a hug and talking her through the situation works absolute wonders. The physical touch of the hug releases endorphins and oxytocin which helps calm her down.

Her Kinesthetic and Interpersonal types of thinking in her top two pillars make her an incredibly sensitive child. She is compassionate and feels others' pain and sorrow and will do everything in her power to help solve their problems. She is also very loyal and serious.

Because we now understand the structure of our own giftings and our children's, our family has a deeper understanding of how we can work together. When you operate in your gift, you free others to operate in theirs.

To help you discover the structure of your gift, I have designed a 210-question Gift Profile to help determine the order of your thought sequence.

At this point, there is no surefire way of measuring precisely how much you use each pillar of thought, but there are ways to get a very good idea and the profile I have developed is one. Even if we used brain scanning and imaging techniques, what we would see on them is not the real-time unique thinking pattern. Instead it would be showing the result of the main thinking pattern that brought a thought into conscious awareness in the first place. These scans would show the main focus of the task, reading or drawing for example, but not the thought process leading up to the task. This is because thinking in real-time is extraordinarily fast. We see the fruit, not the process; however, the fruit reflects the process.

The simple "yes" or "no" answer questions in the Gift Profile have been developed over twenty years – based on my doctoral research and years of clinical experience and research on the science of thought and the brain. These questions are designed to help identify a close approximation of your thought pattern.

Once scored, the Gift Profile will have ranked the Seven Pillars from highest to lowest, showing us the order of your pillars – the structure of your gift. Understanding the structure of your gift helps you understand how you can maximize your gift and if there are any gift-blockers you need to overcome.

If you don't maximize the potential of your structure of thought because of gift-blockers, you can miss great opportunities. In Part Four, we will be discussing gift-blockers and how to recognize and deal with them.

In the meantime, the science of thought is fascinating and an integral part of understanding how your gift operates.

Science of Thought
As you process information, it loops through your Seven Pillars and each loop contributes to a deeper understanding of the information. All the loops start at the front of the brain, then loop over to the dominant type of thought and then back to the frontal lobe. Then the second loop starts from the frontal lobe to the next highest pillar and so on (see diagram on page 46).[8]

What is the result? You use all seven types of thinking in your "hardwired" order – if you don't have gift-blockers, this order is like a well-worn pathway that is a shortcut home.

As you think in the way that your brain was designed to function, your brain kicks into high gear and you operate like a fine-tuned piano with all seven types of thought tuned into thinking "it" through. When this happens, all kinds of great chemicals shoot through your brain and a frenzy of memory building begins!

The firing of electrical impulses through your brain is fast, efficient and organized. The brain is not a conglomerate of interconnected parts but an infinitely integrated and exceptionally organized self-regulating system. The thought circuits in the brain are altered by experience, so the more you think in the way you were designed to think, operating in your gift, the more you develop your brain. In fact, as the proficiency of your brain improves, so does your brain health and intelligence.

As we've reviewed, each one of us has seven steps that our thoughts must sequence through in order to develop and complete a thought loop and process the thought (see diagram on page 46):

1. In development stage one, information comes in through your five senses and activates existing thoughts in your mind. This is experienced as the awareness of gathering information and the activation of thoughts in your mind just on the tip of consciousness.
2. In development stage two, you start to build a temporary memory. You experience this as a thought of new information that you may or may not remember.
3. In development stage three, the information is consolidated. You experience this as thinking, "This is or isn't starting to make sense."
4. In development stage four, as though to confirm accuracy, more connections are invoked. You experience this as a feeling of "This is correct or something is missing," or "It's not quite right or it is almost right."
5. In development stage five, integration into existing circuits starts and continues. You begin to feel you are gaining a level of proficiency.

6. In development stage six, a level of application begins and you experience this as a feeling of "This is meaningful; I can use this or do this."

7. In development stage seven, the thought completes its first cycle. You experience this as "I am starting to get a handle on what this means," or "I really don't understand and need to think this through some more."

Although the steps are the same for each one of us, the area of the brain – the pillar of thought – that is stimulated in each step is different.

Let's look at an example of a real Gift Profile. Remember, this is simply an example and your sequence will be unique to you.

Here is Kim's Gift Profile, the structure of her gift:

1. Linguistic
2. Intrapersonal
3. Interpersonal
4. Musical
5. Visual/Spatial
6. Kinesthetic
7. Logical/Mathematical

When information cycles through Kim's brain, here is the applied process (see diagram on page 46):

1. Development stage one – Linguistic: The information comes in through one of her five senses and activates existing thoughts in her mind. She best absorbs information through words – speaking, writing, reading and seeing words in her mind.

2. Development stage two – Intrapersonal: She starts to build a temporary memory. As her brain begins to introspect and go

"quiet," she will experience this as a thought that she might or might not remember.

3. Development stage three – Interpersonal: As the information is consolidated, Kim might start to share and communicate using interpersonal skills, helping her brain to make sense of her thoughts.

4. Development stage four – Musical: In order to confirm accuracy, more connections are invoked, and Kim may experience this as a very instinctive feeling that something is correct or something is missing, it's not quite right or it is almost right. Because of the musical nature of this type of thought, Kim may tap her foot, or click a pen rhythmically – all of these help her brain to confirm the accuracy of the information.

5. Development stage five – Visual/Spatial: The integration of the new information into existing circuits starts and continues. Kim may experience this as the feeling of a level of proficiency that she sees in her mind's eye.

6. Development stage six – Kinesthetic: At this point, a level of application begins. Kim may experience this through movement – maybe rocking in a chair, tracing her finger along her notes or standing up and walking around – as a feeling of "this is meaningful, I can use this or do this." She is quite literally moving in a focused way at this point.

7. Development stage seven – Logical/Mathematical: The thought completes its first cycle, applying logical reasoning and thinking. Kim may experience this as "I am starting to get a handle on what this means" or "I really don't understand and need to think this through some more." She may create an action plan, written or thought out, on the steps to move forward.

Then, Kim will reopen the thought and go through the process again straight away, and maybe an hour or day or week later, and so on, in order to establish the circuit that she built, and again after that and as many times as she wants or needs or chooses to. It is up to her.

Once the neural circuit becomes established, fewer neurons are required to perform the task and the circuit becomes available to other circuits in an integrative and interconnected way.

Through life, that truth-value, that uniqueness, that gift will be developed to whatever level of intellect you desire. So your intelligence is in whose hands? Yours!

See, God hardwired you to be an incredibly gifted, intelligent person. The level of your gifting, the level of your intelligence that He's given you is developed by using your brain correctly and reaching the level of intelligence that you desire.

If Logical/Mathematical happens to be at the bottom of the order of your gift, and you aren't that great at math, it doesn't matter. If you develop your gifting, the others will naturally follow.

We have had math students who have been failing math. I am thinking of one of my students back in South Africa who was dominant Musical and Kinesthetic thinking and failing math.

He was desperate to play a musical instrument, but his parents wouldn't allow him to until he improved his math grade. Well, I profiled him and showed his parents that the way to get his gift going and pull all of his grades up was through his Musical pillar, since it was the highest. So we got him going on keyboard, we got him playing the drums, we got him singing, and we got him playing in a little band.

I tell you, this child's grades in all subjects skyrocketed. He started getting 70s and 80s. His Linguistic intelligence wasn't very high, but by developing his dominant pillar, he used his gift to pull all the other lagging pillars up. When he was able to fully learn and express himself through his dominant pillar of thinking, all the other areas of thinking just naturally lifted. He may never be a Logical/

Mathematical Einstein, but who cares? He's a Musical Einstein and a happy one at that.

You don't have to be like Einstein to be intelligent; you just need to find your gift so you can reach your full potential.

CHAPTER NINE:
{THE STRUCTURE OF YOUR GIFT}

How our gifting works in brain language is best explained with the understanding that your brain is made up of approximately 100 billion neurons that have the potential to connect 100 trillion times. These highly interconnected neurons are clustered into the Seven Pillars or columns of thinking that stretch from left to right across the brain.

This is the scientific foundation to the unlimited potential of your brain we explored in Part One. With about 100 billion neurons that have the potential to connect about 100 trillion times, your brain has an incredible capacity for thoughts and intelligence (see diagram on page 46).

The borders of these pillars of thinking are not fixed but free-flowing, allowing them to flow into each other, helping each other, especially when the brain has been damaged.

I believe that individuality and giftedness arise out of the different arrangements of the pillars of thinking. This difference is reflected in how the nerve cells fire in the brain.

For example, as the neurons fire in your temporal lobe, where language is processed, and if the arrangement of your pillars indicates that Linguistics is the strongest part of your thought structure, then the firing neurons will be amplified in your temporal lobe.

This amplification will be reflected in a higher level of skill, such as being very eloquent and good with words. As all that's happening, the left and right sides of your brain are being drawn together by the central part of your brain called the corpus callosum and its surrounding hub of thousands of electrical chemical circuits. This is an incredibly "brain healthy" process which develops your intelligence as a bonus.

Using your gift correctly is tremendously rewarding. There are many times in your life so far that you have unconsciously used your gift. Those are the moments when you feel, "Wow! I'm actually quite clever. I understood that. I'm not so bad after all." You've all had those moments, and you should have them. Hopefully, you'll have lots more of them now that you're starting to become more aware of this process.

When you suddenly feel so good that you've understood something, it's evidence for you that your gifting has come into operation and you've used your brain in the way it should be used. Grab that moment, grab that feeling, store it, frame it, put it on ice and make sure that you become consciously aware of that feeling. Use this to help guide you into using your gift as much as you can and recognizing when your gift is blocked.

Your gift – that special piece of eternity, which is your unique way of thinking – operates a bit like dominos. There are seven dominoes representing the Seven Pillars of thinking. As in dominos – you push one, then the next one in line falls, and the next and the next and so on, in that particular order. Your order does not change with experience and maturity, but the interaction between the Seven Pillars of thinking that make up your gifting just gets better with the development of wisdom. So, you stay you, but you improve and become more intelligent. God formed you in a certain way, but it's up to you to use what He has given you; there is no limit to your intelligence, only the limit you set for yourself.

You literally have a pattern of thinking that works in a certain sequential way. Your thought pattern is unique to you like a fingerprint, and you will process and build memory in the distinct way suited to you. As you think, you activate your pattern or the order in which you process information. This is a cycle of thought – we go through a loop of thought approximately 30,000 to 60,000 times a day, which is about 2,000 to 4,000 thought cycles per hour (assuming you sleep around seven to nine hours a day) and about 30-60 thought cycles per minute, averaging out to a thought every 1-2 seconds.

And this is only conscious awareness; underneath this is the Metacognitive nonconscious level where approximately 400 billion bits of information per second are going on, making the above conscious process happen. There are all these incredible workings of the mind, when we are only a touch of eternity![9]

You may cycle through your pillars (gift) in this order:

1. Intrapersonal
2. Interpersonal
3. Linguistic
4. Visual/Spatial
5. Kinesthetic
6. Musical
7. Logical/Mathematical

This would involve a flow of electrical and chemical activity through the different parts of the brain in this order (see diagram on page 46). This would be a cycle of thought.

Now, if we just changed 1 and 2, as in the example below:

1. Interpersonal
2. Intrapersonal

3. Linguistic
4. Visual/Spatial
5. Kinesthetic
6. Musical
7. Logical/Mathematical

This would produce a completely different type of thought pattern, a completely different perception of the world, because this is a completely different gift and a completely different way of thinking. An infinite number of thinking variations could be worked out, each giving rise to another thinking pattern or gift.

Your gift has purpose. Your gift is intentional.

CHAPTER TEN:
{THE GIFT PROFILE}

You are uniquely, fearfully and wonderfully made
(see Psalm 139:14).

The Gift Profile is not a diagnostic test and needs to be used in conjunction with formal testing if problems are identified. This Gift Profile uncovers the structure of your gift, which will help you maximize your gift, discover ways you can improve learning for lasting change, and help you better understand how to relate to others.

When we uncover our gifts, we uncover our purpose – the reason for our intentional design. We also uncover who we are, our "true you." We find that something that no one else can do, and we do it. And the bonus in using our gift is that the brain is wired to be more efficient and our intelligence improves as a result!

This Gift Profile is a neuropsychological questionnaire showing us the structure of how we think. When we find out how we think we can capitalize on this by working with and not against our natural brain-compatible thinking style. This means we can take personal responsibility for developing our gifts, which are housed within our thinking. When we think, we think according to our gifts; we create useful knowledge and develop potential. The more we do this the more the brain grows: the branches, called dendrites, on the brain's neurons have little bumps on them like leaves that grow, change shape and shrink as we experience and think about the world. Research shows that self-regulating your thinking and consequent learning are the way we build our gifts and, consequently, intelligence and wisdom. And we certainly need lots of wisdom to navigate life.[10]

So, our gifts, the way we uniquely think, are not a static entity determined by our genetics and the first few years of our lives but dynamic and continuously growing as we use them, which means our intelligence is dynamic and in our hands.

As we think to understand, we are using our gifts, and this increases the branches and the networking capacity in the brain. These connections in the interlaced neural networks (thought clusters) increase the efficiency of the brain. The great news is that the more we use our gifts, the more connections we make and the more efficient our brains become. The brain continues to change and grow into old age, making it an extremely unique organ both among biological and mechanical structures because it does not wear out!

The message of hope in all this is that, when we continually use our gifts, we can enhance and preserve the brain's powers as we move through life.

In the Gift Profile my aim is to help you find that hope, to show you that you are gifted. When you use your gift, magnificent things happen in your brain and the genius hidden in you will come out. It bears repeating that the Gift Profile is just touching the surface of the magnificence of you.

Once you have filled in and scored the profile (in the upcoming sections) you will find your order of how you uniquely think things through to build thought into the neural networks of the mind. The highest two pillars of thought will obviously stand out as the kick start or dominant thinking loops or cycles. They work hand-in-hand with the other five, which are equally as important.

You are a combination of all seven interacting – not just the top one. So you would not say "I am an Interpersonal thinker;" rather you would say "I start processing with Interpersonal, and then I use Intrapersonal to . . . "

Before you do your own Gift Profile, let's have a look at how these intelligences combine to form a fun example of a Gift Profile.

Einstein died in 1955, but there is a lot written about him, some of which we can use to try to create his profile. We spoke earlier in Part One about the research done on Einstein's brain and how researchers studying his brain found larger areas and more connections showing lots of deep thinking in specific ways and lots of integration of information.

Let's consider *a few* of these facts about Einstein, such as:[11]

- The areas found to have these changes in Einstein's brain dealt with Visual/Spatial cognition, mathematical thought and movement imagery type of thinking.
- He was extremely introspective, judging by the fact that he went on to become a great theoretical physicist at 37.
- In 1905 he wrote five ground-breaking papers that the *Encyclopedia Britannica* indicated had forever changed man's view of the universe.
- He was a great internationalist speaking out eloquently on many topics.
- His sayings and deep thoughts are quoted to this day.
- He did not speak until he was three, probably because early language development was usurped by his amazing math and Visual/Spatial capacities.
- He received excellent results in math and sciences.
- He received less than excellent results in technical subjects, including drawing and geography – in fact, he failed French.
- He taught himself Euclidian geometry and calculus between the ages of eleven and sixteen.
- He played the violin quite well.

We have a picture of a man who had a unique pattern of thinking that he applied, showing multifaceted complexity, creativity and wisdom. He "thought out" the genius inside of himself.

From Einstein's own insight into his thinking, his discoveries were "thought experiments" performed in his imagination. I believe it's this unique thought experience, Einstein's gift, which he used and developed through his life, that resulted in the changes researchers see in his brain and not the other way around. When asked how he achieved what he did in 1905, he said, "I don't know, but I looked up to the heavens and God showed me." How amazing.

Our thoughts are not His thoughts (Isaiah 55:9), but God has graced us with a bit of Him in the unique way we think.

Einstein once said that knowledge is limited but imagination is not. It is through the powers of imagination that we expand our knowledge.

Einstein's experiences highlight the inherent limitations of existing paradigms about thinking and learning. They underscore the importance of seeing people as individuals in educational environments and not making judgments about their intelligence and potential based on how well – or how badly – they are able to do a few exercises in a specific time. It also emphasizes how little you can tell about students from just observing their behavior in the classroom.

It is a bit like when Rabbit went to school. He was so excited that he signed up for all the classes, including swimming lessons. The term started off well and Rabbit was full of passion and enthusiasm. As the term progressed, his grades in hopping, running and jumping were great. However, swimming was a problem, which reflected negatively in his grades. At the end of the term, his teacher commended him on his progress in hopping, running and jumping but was disappointed in his swimming results. She then commented that next term, Rabbit would have to stop running, hopping and jumping lessons and just concentrate on swimming. Well, we can all guess what happened to Rabbit: he drowned.

This is a powerful and poignant analogy of what is happening out there in the storm-tossed sea of education, therapy and life with teachers, therapists, parents and friends so set on improving our weaknesses that they don't support our strengths.

Yet the brain is designed in such a way that its strengths support its weaknesses. In fact, the "weaknesses" should not be seen in a negative light at all. They are simply complementary opposites to strengths, giving people their uniqueness. Now isn't that a much more positive and pleasant way of looking at the whole person?

Yes, it's true. You are truly amazing, and you are about to find out just how marvelously clever you are. To do that, you need to answer some important questions, which include:

- What do you like doing best?
- What kind of activities appeal to you?
- What are you good at?

Just as importantly, you need to know what type of person you really are – how your brain is wired. These questions need answers if you are really going to change the way you do things, live in your gift and make a difference in your life and the world.

Now that you know something about the seven different types of thinking – your gift that exists in your brain – it is time to work out your Gift Profile. After that, you can consider the implications of this on your life and, in particular, the way you think and learn.

11

CHAPTER ELEVEN:
{HOW TO COMPLETE THE GIFT PROFILE}

This Gift Profile has been developed over the past twenty years and is rooted in my theory of Geodesic Learning, which I developed to help understand the science of thought. For schools, businesses, ministries and individuals it has become an extremely useful tool in evaluating the structure of gifting. It is meant to encourage and guide us into realizing that we are all gifted at something, we just have to find it. There is something you can do that no one else can.

The profile is in a questionnaire format, arranged in seven different categories, each of which represents one of the Seven Pillars that make up your gift. Simply select a "yes" or "no" answer to each question. Circle "yes" if you think the question applies to you. Circle "no" if it does not.

Some questions may seem ambiguous, in which case you should follow your "gut instinct," circling "yes" or "no" according to your first reaction. Your immediate, instinctive reaction will be the most accurate.

If you feel that you are gifted in different areas of your life when you are at home, than when you are at the office, you have detected something very interesting at the heart of your gifting.

Each of us has a true-self, and each one of us also has been influenced by our environment and circumstances, adopting skills to function – adapting our gifting to our work situation and environment. So you may wish to complete the Gift Profile twice, once from a personal point of view and once from a professional and/or academic perspective.

Sometimes when people complete the Gift Profile for the first time, they can lose focus because their two roles (professional and personal) have become so intertwined that it becomes hard to separate them. As you complete the Gift Profile, you might find yourself thinking, "I don't really like doing this, but I have had to learn the skill," or "This doesn't come naturally to me, but I have developed this skill over the years."

If you find yourself saying this, then the skill you are evaluating, via the question you are reading, is not natural to you. You would need to circle "no" when you complete the Gift Profile from a personal perspective and "yes" when you complete it from a professional standpoint.

When you first complete the profile, use these questions to guide you:

- What do I like to do? (If you don't like it, don't select it!)
- What comes naturally to me?
- What appeals to me?

The second time you complete the profile, keep the following questions in mind:

- What have I had to develop to perform better academically, professionally and/or experientially? (For example, you may not naturally be organized but have had to train yourself in order to cope with your job or academics.)
- How has a particular skill or quality developed due to the nature of my work life environment or academic demands?
- What is it that I don't like to do but have had to do or have learned to do in my work/learning/teaching/ home environment?

And remember:

- There is no right or wrong answer.
- You are not trying to impress anyone.
- Pure honesty is what is required.
- You are not supposed to score high on everything.

Most of the intelligences will be around 40-70%, a few around 70-80% and two or three might be higher. If you get a high score in most areas, you have either mixed your personal and academic profiles, or you have not been totally honest!

The highest scores, your strengths, focus on your abilities. These questions are just a sampling to give you an idea of where your strengths lie.

Please note, if you'd like your children to complete the Gift Profile, there are developmental aspects to the Gift Profile. The brain goes through growth spurts up to the age of eighteen years, which will affect the results of the profile. For example, in a young child from the ages of approximately five to eight years, the brain is going through a major growth spurt and is therefore still developing.

Over time, as the child's brain grows and matures, the scores will increase, but the dominant pillars will not change, unless a particular skill has been concentrated on and developed, like when piano lessons develop musical intelligence.

Remember that between the ages of eight and eleven, children may try too hard to give the answers they think the person asking the questions wants. So it is helpful to emphasize to younger children that it is good to say "no" to a question because what you are looking for is what they like, not what you as the teacher or mom wants them to like.

In effect, they may play the "school game." Younger children tend to be more natural. You also need to provide lots of examples for each of the questions for younger children.

Fill in your final percentages (blue for personal and red for professional /academic) on the gift combination evaluation chart at the beginning of the next chapter. Now find your highest scores. The easiest way to do this is to rank the scores from highest to lowest. (Remember, they should not all come out high!)

THE GIFT PROFILE QUESTIONNAIRE
Intrapersonal Intelligence

1. I am very aware of all my emotions.   Yes   No

2. I am easily able to express how I feel in detail.   Yes   No

3. I can easily find different ways to express my
    emotions and thoughts.   Yes   No

4. I can sit quietly for hours on my own thinking
    and sorting things out in my own mind.   Yes   No

5. I believe I am very well balanced.   Yes   No

6. I can work independently.   Yes   No

7. I am very organized.   Yes   No

8. I am motivated to set goals for myself
    and to achieve them.   Yes   No

9. I don't need people around me all the time.   Yes   No

10. I prefer to be on my own to being in a group.   Yes   No

11. I enjoy my own company.   Yes   No

12. I am very curious about the deep issues of life and love to ponder their meaning and relevance.   Yes   No

13. I love to philosophize.   Yes   No

14. I am challenged by the purpose of life.   Yes   No

15. It is very important for me to understand my inner experiences.   Yes   No

16. Human rights issues are close to my heart.   Yes   No

17. I am very affected by the plight of others.   Yes   No

18. I am determined to make a difference in life.   Yes   No

19. I have a desire to empower others.   Yes   No

20. I am a very good listener.   Yes   No

21. I only offer advice if asked.   Yes   No

22. I find it very easy to consider a person's problem and to advise him or her.   Yes   No

23. I never impose my ideas on others even though I always have an opinion.   Yes   No

24. I have insight into issues and life in general.		Yes	No
25. I love writing journal entries.		Yes	No
26. I enjoy receiving feedback on my efforts.		Yes	No
27. I prefer to work alone.		Yes	No
28. I often have opinions that set me apart from the crowd.		Yes	No
29. I prefer self-directed learning as in distance learning.		Yes	No
30. I consider myself to have a good self-esteem.		Yes	No

Interpersonal Intelligence

1.	I need people around me a lot.	Yes	No
2.	I form friendships easily.	Yes	No
3.	I keep good friendships for many years.	Yes	No
4.	I recognize that there are many different ways of communicating with others.	Yes	No
5.	I make use of these different ways of communicating.	Yes	No
6.	I find it easy to tune into the needs of others.	Yes	No

7. I am able to perceive the thoughts and feelings of others.   Yes   No

8. I find it easy to counsel and guide people.   Yes   No

9. People tend to come to me for counsel and advice.   Yes   No

10. I like to influence the opinions and/or actions of others.   Yes   No

11. I enjoy participating in collaborative efforts.   Yes   No

12. I am able to assume various roles in a group – from the follower to the leader.   Yes   No

13. I prefer to lead rather than follow in a group.   Yes   No

14. I am quick to understand the verbal and non-verbal communication of a group or of a person.   Yes   No

15. I get on well with my parents, brothers and sisters.   Yes   No

16. I communicate effectively both on a non-verbal and a verbal level.   Yes   No

17. I can easily adapt my behavior and conversation to different groups and environments.   Yes   No

18. I can easily adapt my explanation or
    communication or behavior based on
    the feedback of others.   Yes   No

19. I am very good at mediating.   Yes   No

20. I love mentoring people.   Yes   No

21. I am good at organizing others into
    getting a group project done.   Yes   No

22. I can easily work with people from
    diverse ages and backgrounds.   Yes   No

23. I am a good leader and visionary.   Yes   No

24. I am good at managing people in terms
    of action planning and getting things done.   Yes   No

25. I am good at arguing a point and can
    be convincing.   Yes   No

26. I thrive on attention.   Yes   No

27. I like to be needed.   Yes   No

28. I am good at conflict management.   Yes   No

29. I am a good "solution-finder."   Yes   No

30. I like to generate many perspectives on topics.   Yes   No

Linguistic Intelligence

1. I like using stories to explain something.   Yes   No

2. I like debating in discussions.   Yes   No

3. I enjoy writing poems, stories, legends
   and articles.   Yes   No

4. I would like to write a play.   Yes   No

5. I like telling stories.   Yes   No

6. I like describing events in detail.   Yes   No

7. I like giving presentations.   Yes   No

8. I like leading discussions.   Yes   No

9. I like writing/typing journal entries.   Yes   No

10. I would love to create a talk show
    program for radio or TV.   Yes   No

11. I enjoy writing newsletters.   Yes   No

12. I love using, for example, encyclopedias,
    concordances and thesauruses to expand
    my knowledge.   Yes   No

13. I love inventing catchy slogans or sayings.   Yes   No

14. I like or would enjoy conducting an interview.   Yes   No

15. I use email and text messaging a lot.   Yes   No

16. I enjoy or would enjoy writing a novel
    or long story.   Yes   No

17. I always have something to say and
    enjoy talking.   Yes   No

18. Books and reading materials are very
    important to me.   Yes   No

19. I hear words in my head before I speak,
    read or write.   Yes   No

20. I hear words in my head as I listen to
    someone or when I am watching TV.   Yes   No

21. I would rather listen to the radio or a
    CD than watch TV.   Yes   No

22. I enjoy word and information games
    like Scrabble and Trivial Pursuit.   Yes   No

23. I enjoy entertaining myself and others with
    tongue twisters, puns and nonsense rhymes.   Yes   No

24. I like to use complex vocabulary and
    long sentences.   Yes   No

25. When driving or in a car I pay more
    attention to signs, billboards and anything
    written versus scenery.   Yes   No

26. I prefer subjects like history, literature,
    integrated studies and languages to math,
    science and computer studies.   Yes   No

27. In a conversation, I refer a lot to what I
    have read or heard.   Yes   No

28. I spell well.   Yes   No

29. I have good general knowledge.   Yes   No

30. I ask a lot of questions.   Yes   No

Logical/Mathematical Intelligence

1. Mathematical formulas "talk" to me.   Yes   No

2. I see meaning in numbers.   Yes   No

3. I like designing and conducting experiments.   Yes   No

4. I like creating strategy games like Survivor
   and treasure hunts.   Yes   No

5. I like organizing my time.   Yes   No

6. I like interpreting data.   Yes   No

7. I like hypothesizing and asking "What if?"   Yes   No

8. I like categorizing facts and information.   Yes   No

9. I like describing symmetry and balance.   Yes   No

10. I can always see the pros and cons of a situation.	Yes	No
11. I like planning.	Yes	No
12. I like reasoning things out.	Yes	No
13. I like playing with numbers and doing complex mathematical operations.	Yes	No
14. I like using technology.	Yes	No
15. I can easily compute numbers in my head.	Yes	No
16. My favorite subjects are or were science, math and computer science.	Yes	No
17. I enjoy logical *games* like chess and cards.	Yes	No
18. I enjoy computer games.	Yes	No
19. I enjoy brain teasers.	Yes	No
20. I enjoy problem-solving.	Yes	No
21. I enjoy "What if?" games.	Yes	No
22. My mind searches for patterns and regularities and logical sequences.	Yes	No
23. New developments in science, technology and nature interest me.	Yes	No
24. I like rational explanations for everything.	Yes	No

25. I often think in abstract (wordless, imageless) concepts.	Yes	No
26. I understand and need order.	Yes	No
27. I am immediately aware of logical flaws in a person's argument or conversation.	Yes	No
28. I notice illogical sequences for example, in events or films.	Yes	No
29. I like building puzzles.	Yes	No
30. I love questioning and experimenting.	Yes	No

Kinesthetic Intelligence

1. I need to explore a new environment through touch and movement.	Yes	No
2. I like to touch or handle what I need to learn; I cannot just look at it.	Yes	No
3. I consider myself to be well coordinated.	Yes	No
4. I have a good sense of timing in life, for example, I am always on time and can manage my time.	Yes	No
5. I have a good sense of timing when it comes to physical activities.	Yes	No
6. I am good at arranging furniture in a room and placing decorative items on a table.	Yes	No

7. I enjoy field trips like visiting a museum
or the planetarium.   Yes   No

8. I enjoy participating in plays.   Yes   No

9. I enjoy physical strategy games like Catches,
Stuck in the Mud and treasure hunts.   Yes   No

10. I notice when people have not color
coordinated their clothes, fabrics or
styles correctly.   Yes   No

11. I like symmetry in a room, for example,
putting two identical potted plants on
either side of a couch.   Yes   No

12. I am aware of and concerned about my
physical health so I exercise regularly and
try to eat a healthy, balanced diet.   Yes   No

13. I find it easy to participate in a group activity
that involves a coordinated sequence of
movements such as aerobics and dancing.   Yes   No

14. I am good at activities involving dexterity
with my hands, like sewing.   Yes   No

15. I like doing things like pottery
and woodcarving.   Yes   No

16. I find it easy to create new forms in
a sport, for example, a new type of
dance or a new version of basketball.   Yes   No

17. I have good ball skills and can therefore play soccer, baseball, football and tennis.   Yes   No

18. I have excellent hand-eye coordination and therefore am good at tennis, softball, racquetball and basketball.   Yes   No

19. I am a good cyclist.   Yes   No

20. I love to run for exercise.   Yes   No

21. I love to take part in marathons.   Yes   No

22. I prefer individual to group sports.   Yes   No

23. I love movement and sport, but I am not that proficient in any particular sport.   Yes   No

24. I love swimming.   Yes   No

25. I find it difficult to sit still for long periods of time, especially in a classroom environment.   Yes   No

26. I often feel compelled to move about in order to help myself not lose concentration.   Yes   No

27. I find that I need to move in some way – even if it is wiggling – when I am learning and building memory.   Yes   No

28. I like making models of things with play dough or clay.   Yes   No

29. I really enjoy watching sports – live and on TV – and recognize and appreciate the skill involved. Yes No

30. I like using my hands and body movement when I am talking. Yes No

Musical Intelligence

1. I can easily read body language. Yes No

2. I find it easy to pick up the nuances in someone's speech, for example, whether he or she is sarcastic, angry, irritated or worried. Yes No

3. I find myself listening and responding to a variety of sounds including the human voice, environmental sounds, sounds in nature and music. Yes No

4. I enjoy music and find myself needing music in the learning environment. Yes No

5. I will often create my own rhythm if I can't hear music, especially when I am concentrating, for example, clicking my pen, tapping my foot or rocking in my chair rhythmically. Yes No

6. I find myself responding to music by humming along. Yes No

7. I find myself responding to music
    by moving in time to the music.   Yes   No

8. I find music and singing make me
    feel various emotions.   Yes   No

9. If I watch gymnastics or ballet or
    dancing or any sport, I can "hear"
    the music in the body movements.   Yes   No

10. I recognize different types of musical
    styles and genres and cultural variations.   Yes   No

11. I find the role music has played and
    continues to play in human life fascinating.   Yes   No

12. I collect CDs and mp3s of different types
    of music.   Yes   No

13. I have the ability to sing.   Yes   No

14. I play one or more musical instruments.   Yes   No

15. I am able and like to analyze and critique
    musical selections.   Yes   No

16. I often am able to interpret what a composer
    is communicating through music.   Yes   No

17. I remember the titles and the words of songs.   Yes   No

18. I can hear a song once or twice and then
    sing most of it.   Yes   No

19. I have a desire to create, or I have created
a musical instrument.   Yes   No

20. I like music.   Yes   No

21. I would love to be (or I am already) a
sound engineer, conductor or musician.   Yes   No

22. I read music.   Yes   No

23. I like musical games, for example, karaoke.   Yes   No

24. I often tap or hum while working or when
learning something new.   Yes   No

25. I like whistling and often do.   Yes   No

26. I often have intuitive hunches.   Yes   No

27. I can easily "read between the lines."   Yes   No

28. I can "read" people easily.   Yes   No

29. I am not easily misled.   Yes   No

30. I am somewhat cynical.   Yes   No

Visual/Spatial Intelligence

1. I think in 3-D, for example, I can easily mentally
move or manipulate objects in space to see how
they will interact with other objects, such as
gears turning parts of machinery.   Yes   No

2. I like to produce and can easily
   understand graphic information, for
   example, using graphs or charts to
   explain concepts.   Yes   No

3. I can easily navigate my way through
   space, for example, when I'm moving
   through apertures, moving a car through
   traffic, parking a car, etc.   Yes   No

4. I can easily read a road map.   Yes   No

5. I like building blocks, origami objects,
   Lego, models and bridges.   Yes   No

6. I like building puzzles, especially big ones. Yes   No

7. I like creating photo collages
   and scrapbooking.   Yes   No

8. I like creating PowerPoint presentations.   Yes   No

9. I like taking photos or creating videos
   of special occasions.   Yes   No

10. I like designing posters/murals/bulletin boards. Yes   No

11. I find myself visualizing (pictures and imaging)
    a lot especially when I am listening and trying
    to understand.   Yes   No

12. I can easily remember large chunks of information
    (for short periods of time) just from reading. Yes   No

13. I like creating complex "architecture" type drawings.   Yes   No

14. I would love to make (or love making) a film or an advertisement.   Yes   No

15. I appreciate and notice variation in color, size and shape, for example, I notice the colors, furniture and interior design in rooms.   Yes   No

16. I naturally color code, for example, Sunday is red, and Monday is blue.   Yes   No

17. I like board games like Monopoly and Trivial Pursuit.   Yes   No

18. I like and am fairly good at producing various art forms such as illustrations, drawings, sketches, paintings and sculpture.   Yes   No

19. I like using technology, such as computers.   Yes   No

20. I like to do presentations and lectures or teach using computers, data projectors and overhead projectors.   Yes   No

21. I like writing on a board or flipchart when I am explaining something, lecturing or teaching.   Yes   No

22. I see clear visual images of what I am thinking or hearing when I close my eyes.   Yes   No

23. I have vivid dreams.   Yes   No

24. I can easily find my way around and only need to go to a place once and will easily find my way back again.   Yes   No

25. I like drawing and doodling especially when on the phone or when listening to a lecture where I have to concentrate.   Yes   No

26. I prefer not to look at a lecturer or teacher's face when I am trying to concentrate as this distracts me.   Yes   No

27. I find it easier to learn when I can see and observe.   Yes   No

28. I often use visual images as an aid to recall detailed information.   Yes   No

29. I can easily fold a piece of paper into a complex shape and visualize its new form.   Yes   No

30. I find it easy to see things – both concrete and linguistic – in different ways or from new perspectives, for example, detecting one form hidden in another or seeing the "other angle" of a problem.   Yes   No

12

CHAPTER TWELVE: {WHAT YOUR GIFT PROFILE SAYS ABOUT YOU}

If the human brain were so simple that we could understand it, we would be so simple that we couldn't.
– Emerson M. Pugh

Fill in your scores from the questionnaire in the table below to create your Gift Profile.

THE ORDER OF THE GIFT	1st Profile (Personal)	1st Profile (Professional)
Intrapersonal Intelligence		
Interpersonal Intelligence		
Linguistic Intellingence		
Logical/Mathematical Intelligence		
Kinesthetic Intelligence		
Musical Intelligence		
Visual/Spatial Intelligence		

Sometimes, the way you think best – the way your brain is really wired – may be very different from the way you thought you processed.

Alternatively, you may now be starting to understand better why you think and do what you do. You can now move on to what this all means to you specifically and what you can start doing with the information right now.

You have also moved away from the common, misguided perception of intelligence as a single, universal sign of human competence, to the more accurate recognition that our capacities as humans are the product of seven distinct types of thought – the Seven Pillars.

Consider for a moment the following questions:

- In what ways are you gifted?
- Can you create a magnificent piece of artwork from a blank canvas?
- Do you sing or play a musical instrument in a way that touches the hearts of those listening to you?
- Do you inspire people by your vision and lead them to greater heights?
- Do you write page-turning novels or poetry that moves mountains?
- Do you offer advice that puts you in the category of a sage?
- Is your mental math so precise that others are in awe of you?
- Do you play tennis or any other sport so well that everyone is amazed at your mastery?

Each of these questions represents the development of different forms of thinking in action. I remind you that the questions are not totally comprehensive – you would need thousands of questions to cover all the sub skills in one pillar of thought.

The recognition of the fact that we are all so uniquely made and that no one is better than anyone else is the first step toward harnessing the powers of your intellect. Armed with the knowledge of which pillar is dominant in you, which starts the thinking process, you can begin to use your other forms of thinking along with this optimally, as in the example of Einstein.

You can also start making your contribution to a really important task: creating "intelligence-fair" and "true-you fair" ways of perceiving each other, our children, our colleagues, our learners, our educators and our bosses.

A wise person once said: "Every journey begins with a single step." That is true of this next stage of your journey toward becoming more intelligent: assessing your Gift Profile, beginning to think about your dominant pillar.

The Harmony of Thinking

The truth is that there is no one pillar superior to the others, though some, such as the Logical/Mathematical pillar, are universal.[12] Others, such as language and reading abilities, are culturally specific. Within each type of thought, there are steps ranging from novice to expert.

However, there are enormous individual differences in the speed at which a person passes from novice to mastery and, of course, differences in each person's gift combination. There is also the developmental sequence to take into consideration.

But because one type of thinking is stronger or more dominant in you does not mean the others are weak. They are simply less dominant and work with the dominant. They cannot function properly in isolation. Their strength comes from their interaction.

You have to have all seven working in combination to make up your gift or you would not be able to function normally in daily life. You also need all seven working together through your dominant pillars in order to promote emotional intelligence or EQ.

For example, when you are sitting in a restaurant having a conversation with a friend, your Linguistic type of thinking is dominating; when you tune into each other and take turns in talking, your Interpersonal thinking is operating; your ability to sit on the chair without falling off is your Visual/Spatial and Kinesthetic thinking working; the appreciation of the atmosphere and ambience of the restaurant is a combination of your Intrapersonal and Musical thinking (your Musical thinking will also be helping you interpret the nuances in your friend's voice); your Kinesthetic thinking will help you when you maneuver your way through the chairs and tables in the restaurant to the restroom; your Logical/Mathematical thinking will be operating as you move through the logical steps in solving your friend's crisis; and finally, your Visual/Spatial thinking will help you appreciate the well-coordinated design of the restaurant.

To grow as a human being and to use your innate potential, you need to move away from what I call a "disability focus" – focusing on your weaknesses and forgetting about your strengths. You need to focus on what you can do, rather than what you think you can't do. When you do that, you will find that your non-dominant thinking will naturally grow stronger. We also need to stop desiring someone else's gift and rather focus on and develop our own.

The fact is, your brain is designed in such a way that your strengths support your weaknesses. That's why weaknesses should not be seen in a negative light. They are the flip side of your strengths and can therefore be renamed as non-dominances. Like day, they follow night. Like failure, they give you opportunities to learn, to grow and to succeed. They are part of what makes you unique.

An overemphasis on trying to overcome weaknesses creates much of the unhappiness in our world. It is much like trying to force the proverbial square peg into a round hole. It is the reason so many people seek but don't find meaning in their lives.

Unfortunately, one of the most concerning aspects in traditional schooling systems is that some educators are blissfully unaware of the existence of multiple thinking intelligences in their learners. They teach as if all their students' brains process information in exactly the same way.

The results of this can be nothing short of tragic. Students are made to focus on their weaknesses and are not given the freedom to focus on their strengths, because educators and parents, most likely through no fault of their own, have no idea what their students' strengths are. In many cases, they may not even acknowledge that some of their students have any strengths at all, especially if they happen not to be strong in Logical/Mathematical and Linguistic domains – the so-called "school intelligences."

Another enduring myth about thinking and intelligence has to do with who is creative. Most people may have been taught that those with a dominant Visual/Spatial or Musical thinking are only the truly creative ones. Children and adults are labeled as "creative" if they happen to be artistic or musical in conventional senses.

Yet creativity is expressed through all the Seven Pillars. Most people are creative within one or two forms of thought only; therefore, a good plumber is as creative as someone who can paint a portrait.

Few people would easily associate analytical thinking with being creative, yet there are many examples where it is extremely creative. The great Italian artist Leonardo da Vinci, for example, was clearly artistic. He left behind many masterpieces to attest to his prodigious artistic talents. He also had strong Logical/Mathematical thinking, which many educators would not easily attach with the idea of creativity. He designed the first helicopter, completed and recorded the first anatomical dissection, and sang like an angel.

Einstein is another example. He was clearly gifted mathematically and logically, yet he was certainly creative. He may not have produced works of art like da Vinci, but he gave us many amazing insights into the universe around us and the way it works. His ability to visualize was incredible. No one would ever describe Einstein as lacking in creativity.

Each one of us is a special part of this wonderfully unique puzzle that is life. To find our place in it and to be the right piece that fits harmoniously into the whole puzzle, we need to do what we are designed to do. Sadly, many people don't do that and end up living a life with tragic consequences, much like Rabbit, who we discussed earlier.

Ultimately, when all seven types of thinking are allowed to work together, you begin to operate in your gift and move toward knowing, being and accepting who you really are. You move away from being what you are not and stop trying to live up to other people's expectations and quit feeling like you have to put up fronts or façades. You move toward who you really are. This is what I call your truth-value.

When you live according to your truth-value, not only will you become much more intelligent, but you also become much more likely to live a happy, fulfilled life. In other words, you will become more emotionally intelligent, which is another of the amazing benefits of this paradigm of Geodesic Learning.

Now look at your Gift Profile. Where are your highest scores? Compare the differences between the personal (the real you) and the professional/academic (how you have had to grow and change because of the demands of academics or work) in your strongest types of thought (see page 119).

Remember that it is normal to have one dominant pillar, though some people may have two or three. Having more than one dominant type of thinking is not a sign of greater intelligence, though; it's merely a different variation of the Seven Pillars.

Reflect on these results. The following questions may help you:

- Which type of thinking is your highest type of thinking score?
- Which are the second and third highest? These are your supporting non-dominant types of thought.
- Does this reflect how you perceive yourself?
- Are there differences between the personal and professional/academic scores?
- If there are differences, can you see that the dominant types of thought have helped raise the others?
- Were your areas of strength ever nurtured as a child?
- What kinds of gifts do you see in your family, peers, colleagues or students?
- What does this all mean to you?

As you work with your Gift Profile, you need to think on two levels.

First, you need to find out what form of thinking is strongest in you; then you should begin to appreciate the need to develop interaction between your other types of thinking, all seven of them. This will allow your stronger types of thinking to dominate, and just as importantly, it will enhance the non-dominant types of thinking to work through your first and second dominant pillars, which will improve your overall thinking skills and intelligence.

Your gift will be released and you will start to realize your potential. True, nature and nurture play a role in your neural hardwiring and intellectual potential, but only to provide the framework; it's up to you to develop your gift, and the sky is the limit! So the way you think and the choices you make are more powerful than you may have thought.

Your gift is a dynamic growing part of who you are – not a predetermined mold.

The final part of the equation for the improvement of thinking and intelligence is you. You and your attitude – your freedom of choice in response to circumstances – will determine how your gift develops. It is within your grasp.

This means harnessing all your types of thinking so they can work in harmony together. The more you allow them to work together, the more synergy there will be between the two sides of your brain and the more intelligent you will be on many levels. When you allow your Seven Pillars to work together in the natural design – your gift – you become a person filled with wisdom.

You become someone who is able to:

- plan
- strategize
- imagine
- listen
- reason
- guide
- reflect
- follow

- evaluate
- intellectualize
- analyze
- actualize
- consider
- create

And when you can do all of the above well (most of the time!) you will become a good:

- leader
- parent
- follower
- friend
- educator
- spouse
- manager
- professional
- Anything you want to be!
- In other words, you will be a success!

Now here are some guidelines to help you harness the power of your gift.

Intrapersonal Thinking

If the Intrapersonal type of thought is your dominant thinking, you think deeply inside yourself. You build memory through being given quiet time to evaluate the knowledge you are receiving. You don't work well in a group or through discussions with others. You won't cope well in conventional learning environments.

You can enhance your Intrapersonal thinking when you:

- Develop your self-awareness by listening to and becoming aware of what you are thinking.
- Analyze your intuition when it has proven to be correct.
- Develop your senses, which increases your awareness.
- Have quiet time alone.
- Write down your dreams.
- Associate new and unique ideas with old ideas.
- See things from different points of view.
- Respond as fully as you can to aesthetically appealing objects.
- Solve problems and find solutions.
- Always see a situation as a challenge, no matter how bad, and find solutions to solve it.
- Be honest with yourself.
- Make the effort to listen deeply to others and to what they are really trying to say.
- Use the 5 Step Switch On Your Brain™ Learning Process (see the Recommended Reading for this program).

Interpersonal Thinking

If the Interpersonal type of thinking is dominant, then you think by:

- Bouncing ideas off other people.
- Building memory through interactive discussion with others.
- You will cope well in a conventional school or learning environment that allows sufficient time for talking to others.

You can enhance your Interpersonal thinking when you:

- Do group work.
- Retell stories or tales.

- Use a thesaurus.
- Practice involving a group in your presentation or lesson and tuning into others.
- Practice making people feel at ease in challenging situations.
- Spend time with people.
- Listen without interrupting and planning your own response.
- Listen twice as much as you talk.
- Put yourself in another's position and try to think how they think.
- Take a presentation skills course.
- Play "What if?" games.
- Take the time to coach or mentor others in something you are good at.
- Use the 5 Step Switch On Your Brain™ Learning Process.

Linguistic Thinking

If your Linguistic type of thinking is dominant, you build memory through words – spoken and written. You need to talk, ask questions, repeat statements and write down thoughts while learning and concentrating.

It is true that no one form of thinking is more important than another, but language is a universal means of communication and we all benefit by developing this form of intelligence and taking advantage of it.

The interesting fact about this form of intelligence is that it is bright and strong in all of us – the proof is that we learned to speak before we had a single formal lesson. The problem for many of us is that after this first fantastic burst of learning as babies and toddlers, our development of this intelligence can slow down. This might happen because at school we may become bored and lose interest in learning when we are forced to learn in ways that don't come naturally to us.

Your Linguistic type of thinking is based on the ability to play with the 26 letters of the alphabet, as they are the foundation of language. The more you increase your capacity to juggle them, the more you will see the relationship between them and the more intelligent you will be.

You enhance your Linguistic thinking when you:

- Read, read and read some more. This is the quickest and most effective way of building Linguistic thinking. Read a variety of literature, from the newspaper to novels, news magazines and even comics! Read across a variety of different subjects.
- Increase your vocabulary by learning one new word a day. Within a year, you will have increased your vocabulary by 365 words. Practice using these words in different contexts.
- Apply effective reading techniques to improve your concentration and comprehension.
- Play word games like Trivial Pursuit, Scrabble, Cluedo and General Knowledge.
- Do crossword puzzles.
- Learn a new language.
- Use the 5 Step Switch On Your Brain™ Learning Process.

Logical/Mathematical Thinking

If your Logical/Mathematical pillar is strongest, you think by reasoning. You build memory through analyzing. You need to quantify and ask questions until you understand. You will cope well in conventional schools or learning environments because their educational system is based heavily on this type of thinking.

You enhance your Logical/Mathematical thinking when you:

- Practice estimating.
- Practice remembering statistics, for example, on your favorite sports team.
- Become aware of how you use numbers automatically on a daily basis. For example, how much time is left till lunch or before work is over etc.
- Use numbers to rank, organize and prioritize other numbers.
- Play mental calculation games. For example, if you are a passenger in a car, add up the numbers you see on registration plates of other vehicles on the road.
- Use your calculator as a training device and not a crutch!
- Break apart information you want to remember.
- Play games that are an effective "mind sport," such as Backgammon, Chess or Bridge.
- Make stories with numbers – let them talk to you.
- Use the 5 Step Switch On Your Brain™ Learning Process.

Kinesthetic Thinking

If the Kinesthetic type of thought dominates, then you will think in movement and through your senses. You build memory through sensory perceptions and movement. You essentially think by seeing, touching and moving materials, which requires externalizing your mental processes. You must be allowed to see, feel, hear, touch, manipulate and move when learning and concentrating, or the information will not absorb into your brain. This form of externalized thinking has several advantages. The sensory information literally provides "food for thought." In addition, you experience a positive sense of action in actually doing something.

Conventional schooling environments make learning especially difficult, if not impossible for you to achieve. They can often be hellish. However, some simple changes will make all the difference.

For example, you enhance your Kinesthetic thinking when you:

- Sit on a ball instead of a chair when learning.
- Stretch frequently.
- Do drama, including formal theater, role-play and simulations.
- Do creative movement, dance and stretching routines.
- Engage in small manipulative tasks, for example, using flash cards and stamps.
- Make things.
- Play games such as scavenger hunts and Twister.
- Learn to play or make a musical instrument.
- Take up pottery or woodcarving.
- Use the 5 Step Switch On Your Brain™ Learning Process.

Musical Thinking

If the Musical type of thinking is dominant, you think via rhythm, melodies and intuition. You build memory through rhythm and must be allowed to create this in any situation where you are learning and concentrating. Not surprisingly, this makes conventional school environments less than optimal for you. Some schools may think they are better than others, simply because they offer Music as a subject. That misses the point of Geodesic Learning in more ways than one and mostly because it restricts the stimulation of Musical intelligence to one session.

The mere existence of music lessons does not mean that Musical thinking is properly stimulated in learners. The truth is that few schools pay much attention to how music can enhance learning in all subject areas and few schools would think of having the right kind of music in the background for many different types of learning situations.

Yet there is a powerful, scientifically established link between music and our emotions that is responsible for memory building, both strong and weak. The strong emotional component of music allows it to add depth to our perceptions.

It is true that there are critical ages for developing sensitivity to sound and pitch, which are between the ages of four and six. During this time, musical stimulation can provide the basis for future musical ability. If you have missed these, it doesn't mean that music is lost to you forever. You don't have to go on to be a budding Mozart or even a rock star to use your Musical intelligence.

You enhance your Musical type of thinking when you:

- Play classical music in the background when working.
- Have musical instruments (or make them) available and play them periodically.
- Do aerobic routines to music.
- Tap a rhythm with your feet in time to your fingers typing on the computer.
- Sing or hum while you work, even if it's under your breath so as not to disturb others.
- Read poetry.
- Pretend you are a disc jockey while you learn or work.
- Be aware of using inflection in your voice and notice the inflection in other people's voices.
- Make an effort to read body language.
- Listen to your intuition.
- Use the 5 Step Switch On Your Brain™ Learning Process.

Visual/Spatial Thinking

If your Visual/Spatial type of thinking is dominant, you think in images and pictures. You build memory through imagery and imagination and need to imagine and visualize while learning and concentrating.

You may not have fared that well in traditional schools in the past. Luckily for you, though, conventional educational environments have begun using more visual and spatial elements in learning. It remains true, though, that ordinary classroom situations are not ideal learning environments for you. You may find looking at someone while concentrating and learning very distracting, so you can't learn optimally just by sitting still and listening to an educator or lecturer. Your instinctive way of thinking almost literally abandons language and enters into abstract modes of thought. It involves various related skills, such as visual discrimination, recognition, projection, mental imagery, spatial reasoning and image manipulation.

Only about 30% of adults and 40% of children are Visual/Spatial dominant. It is therefore not accurate to say that everything we see in our heads is in pictures. When visual learning dominates in both children and adults, visual strategies should always be a part of the learning process as they encouage mental operations not usually performed in a verbal mode.

You enhance your Visual/Spatial type of thinking when you:

- Read and create your own cartoons.
- Examine advertisements and billboards.
- Use poster displays in your office or class to help you think and express ideas.
- Work with flow charts.
- Use mnemonic systems, such as the Roman Room technique, body parts, numbers and rhyme systems to remember, plan and make up linked stories.

- Draw pictures or doodle when thinking.
- Practice differentiating between colors.
- Take an art course.
- Practice developing your visual memory by doing the da Vinci exercise, that is, stare at a complex object, memorize it, then close your eyes and try to recall it in as much detail as possible.
- Play imaginative games.
- Build complex Lego structures.
- Take a robotics course.
- Use the 5 Step Switch On Your Brain™ Learning Process.

Clearly, as you work with and strengthen your dominant form of thinking, you will begin to appreciate that all seven types of thinking do exist in all of us, in our gifts, on every level and in every culture. The gift may be dormant, but it is there, waiting to come alive. Your gift will awaken when you discover it.

Now that you better understand the structure of your gift, in Part Three we'll look at what might be standing in the way of your greatest potential – your greatest purpose.

PART THREE: Choosing to Live Out Your Gift

INTRODUCTION

"He has made everything beautiful in its time. He also has planted eternity in men's hearts and minds [a divinely implanted sense of a purpose working through the ages which nothing under the sun but God alone can satisfy], yet so that men cannot find out what God has done from the beginning to the end"
(Ecclesiastes 3:11 AMP).

I hope that you are filled with expectancy and excitement because you are starting to understand how you make decisions, how you learn and how your gift is structured. Along the way, you have probably also learned more about your spouse, your children, your friends and neighbors, and maybe even your boss!

Now when you wonder, "Does anyone out there understand me?" you can see in Scripture that God does – He created you with care. Now you can better understand yourself – how you were created with intention, a purpose and greatness.

In Part Three, we will take the structure of your gift one step further and explore what may be keeping you from your potential, from your true self, the person God created you to be.

Although our perfect God has designed us in perfection, we live in a fallen world. What was meant for good can easily turn toxic, through toxic thoughts, toxic words and toxic actions.

Life happens. People hurt us, and sometimes we hurt other people.

Toxic seeds, even little seeds, can start to grow gift-blockers, which can block your gift.

When you have a gift-blocker – or more likely gift-blockers – in action, attitude is affected. An attitude isn't just a flippant word or a flitting mood. In science, an attitude is a cluster of thoughts with emotions attached.

In your brain, you have millions of these clusters of thoughts, each with its own emotions. These clusters of thoughts combine to form one overriding attitude that describes you.

Because each cluster of thoughts triggers specific emotions, individual attitudes will emerge as the individual thought clusters are activated. We can have a combination of healthy and toxic attitudes all mixed in together. Essentially, attitude is the "flavor" of our thoughts.

There are three principles operating when we talk about attitudes:

1. Attitude cannot be hidden.
2. Attitude is the state of your spirit and mind that influences your choices, which in turn influences your words and your behavior.
3. Attitude is tangible – we can feel it because of the chemicals that are released.

A Well-Developed Toxic Thought: A Schematic Representation

A Well-Developed Healthy Thought: A Schematic Representation

These three principles indicate that we can use our attitudes to help identify and unblock the gift-blockers.

Here's how it works: Your gift is your unique way you think through the Seven Pillars of thought.

Both the toxic thoughts (toxic attitudes) and non-toxic thoughts (healthy attitudes) "filter" information, adding either a negative or positive flavor to them. Consequently, these filters either distort or enhance the thinking process, blocking or unblocking the effective operation of the gift.

If you have a toxic thought while you are processing in your own unique way, you have to "push" the information through the toxic thoughts (toxic attitude) in your brain as you are looping through the Seven Pillars.

Toxic thoughts and their tangible bad attitude become gift-blockers. The result is that gift-blockers inhibit our ability to think and operate in wisdom and our overall health in mind and body.

We have to adopt the guiding principle: We can't control our circumstances (life, people), but we can choose to control our reaction (attitude) to the circumstances.

In the next chapter, I am going to discuss attitude in more detail, helping you to identify its tangible aspects and how to recognize them when they get toxic.

Then you will see how to overcome these toxic gift-blockers.

You *can* walk in the gift God has given you – with confidence and purpose.

13

CHAPTER THIRTEEN:
{LOVE AND FEAR}

As we've learned, an attitude is a cluster of thoughts with emotional flavor, and every type of emotion has one of only two roots – love or fear.[1] Love and fear are the root emotions, and all other emotions grow from these.

For example, out of love flow joy, peace, happiness, patience, kindness, gentleness, faithfulness, self-control, compassion, calmness, inspiration, excitement, hope, anticipation and satisfaction. Out of fear flow hate, anger, bitterness, rage, irritation, unforgiveness, unkindness, worry, self-pity, envy, jealousy, obsession and cynicism.

The discovery that love and fear cannot coexist in our brains is revolutionary. In fact, scientists have researched the anatomy and physiology of love and fear right down to a molecular, genetic and epigenetic level that can be described in detail.

They have found a deeper system in the brain concerned with positive love emotions and negative fear emotions. They have discovered that these two systems cannot coexist, that at any one conscious moment, we will be operating in one or the other for each cluster of thoughts we think.[2]

Love Tree

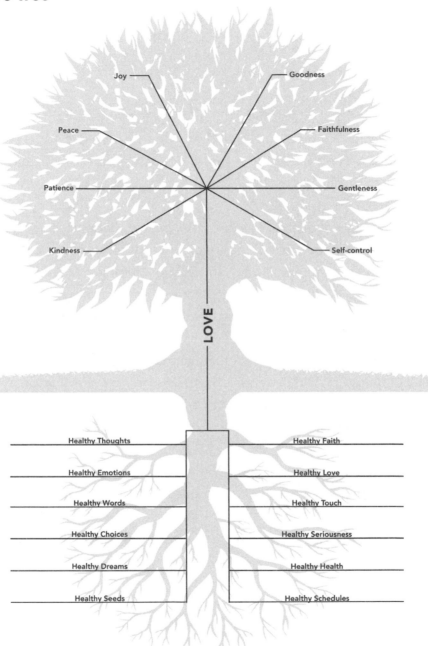

Joy — Goodness

Peace — Faithfulness

Patience — Gentleness

Kindness — Self-control

LOVE

Healthy Thoughts — Healthy Faith

Healthy Emotions — Healthy Love

Healthy Words — Healthy Touch

Healthy Choices — Healthy Seriousness

Healthy Dreams — Healthy Health

Healthy Seeds — Healthy Schedules

Fear Tree

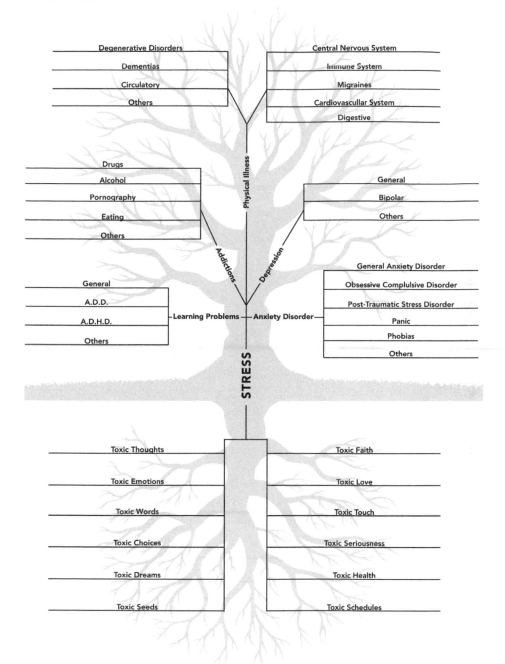

Science is showing us that there is a massive "unlearning" of negative toxic thoughts when we operate in love. The brain releases a chemical called oxytocin, which literally melts away the negative toxic thought clusters so that rewiring of new non-toxic circuits can happen. This chemical also flows when we trust and bond and reach out to others. Love literally wipes out fear![3]

We also have another amazing chemical called dopamine that works with oxytocin. It flows as we expect and anticipate something. It also puts us on heightened alert to build new memories as we imagine helping someone do well in a test or restore a relationship, for example. It gives us a thrilling surge of energy and excitement and confidence and motivation to carry on.

And then as we actually help someone do well in the test or restore the relationship, endorphins and serotonin are released that make us feel great. So when we do good things and reach out in love, God blesses us by helping our brain detox and increase our motivation and wisdom, helping us negotiate life more successfully.[4]

We see this scientific discovery confirmed in Scripture:

"There is no fear in love [dread does not exist], but full-grown (complete, perfect) love turns fear out of doors and expels every trace of terror! For fear brings with it the thought of punishment, and [so] he who is afraid has not reached the full maturity of love [is not yet grown into love's complete perfection]" (1 John 4:18 AMP).

Scientists have shown that when we are in a fear mode we will get caught in a cycle of chemical and neurological responses that dominate and dictate the choices we make and the reactions we set in motion. We will be at the mercy of the environment, the reactions of our body and the toxic memories of the past. Our gift will be blocked and our true-self will vanish. We will quite literally be at the mercy of the effect instead of initiating the cause.[5]

As we learned, in the depths of our nonconscious mind (I call this the Metacognitive level) where about 400 billion actions per second are being performed, we have billions of existing thought clusters with their emotions attached giving their specific attitude "flavor."[6] This is so important to understand, because these thought clusters are referenced and some made conscious every time a new thought starts to form, helping our brains make sense of new information. So when we are exposed to or think about something toxic, and there are thought clusters attached that have toxic emotions attached, they will set in motion a chemical cascade, launching your mind and body into stress mode.

Normally incoming information goes through a certain route as it enters the brain passing through structures as the information is being processed to creatively add to your knowledge.

Some of the important structures involved in this route are the thalamus, which acts like a transmitter station, the amygdala, which is like a library holding emotional perceptions, and the cingulate cortex, which is in the conscious evaluative part of the brain. This route allows incoming information to be received, appraised and evaluated, and the appropriate best and healthiest response from the body to be generated.

We also have an area in the brain called the corpus striatum that is directly involved because it is activated for positive reinforcement and gives us the experience of feeling good, safe and filled with self-confidence. At all costs, this system tries to keep the brain and body calm, peaceful and feeling good, filled with self-confidence and esteem. When the striatum is activated, we get the positive sensation of feeling safe and filled with confidence.

When it's not activated, we do not get this reinforcement of feeling safe. Interestingly enough, the corpus striatum is the area activated by cocaine and other addictive drugs, which highjack this positive reinforcing neural system, making a person feel good and enticing him to use the drug or addictive substance more often.[7]

However, despite the powerful chemicals released by our bodies, we must never forget that greater is He that is in you than he that is in this world (1 John 4:4). God has given you the ability to break free from any addiction. I discuss this in the next chapter.

Just as drugs highjack this positive reinforcing system, so do the "gift-blockers," those toxic thought clusters hiding in the depths of your nonconscious mind, just waiting for the opportunity to highjack your thinking and the neurological pathway of love.

Gift-blockers can also become addictive: How many times have you caught yourself thinking about an issue or event over and over as though you can't let go?

Fear

As we have learned, fear is powerful. It affects us deeply, and we handle it one of three ways:

- We control the fear with conscious cognitive evaluation.
- We become dominated by the unconscious toxic thoughts throwing the body into stress.
- Conscious cognitive evaluation is involved, and instead of controlling fear, we make it worse.

The latter situation, concentrating on the fear, can bring about a fearful state even in the absence of the actual fear stimulus. This is what happens in post-traumatic stress disorder (PTSD) where the memory of a trauma can invoke a response in people that is as real as when it happened, even if the trauma occurred years ago.

The attitudes – cluster of thoughts with the emotion attached – are producing the chemicals for anxiety and worry even though a person is no longer in threatening circumstances.[8] The thoughts about the toxic occurrence, not the actual toxic occurrence, set off the stress response. If we worry every day about what might happen, we create an attitude of uneasiness, which creates the stress response. And this stress response will produce toxic fruit (see images on pages 144 and 145 of the Fear and Love Trees).[9]

It is actually very interesting that scientists call this a "learned" fear because fear is *not* a natural part of how we were created. Fear is a distorted love circuit. We were created for love and all that goes with it, but we have *learned* to fear.[10]

The real pathway – the neurological "love" pathway – is consciously evaluating the toxic fear thought cluster and then choosing to hand the situation to God, not fear. When we do this, the corpus striatum will be activated, all the correct neurotransmitters and peptides and hormones will be secreted, and we will feel good and be able to rejoice despite the circumstances, like it says in James 1:2, "Consider it wholly joyful, my brethren, whenever you are enveloped in or encounter trials of any sort or fall into various temptations" (AMP.).

What we need to remember is this: A thought has an emotional component attached to it, like a "chemical signature."[11] Every time we think, we make chemicals that produce feelings and reactions in the body. Clusters of electrical thoughts with these chemical messengers create our attitudes. We express our attitudes – love or fear – through what we first think and then through the choices we make, which dictate what we say and do. When you add either love or fear emotions to a thought cluster and give it a unique flavor, then it becomes an attitude.

A bad attitude is proof that you are not operating in your gift. A good attitude is proof you are operating in your gift.[12]

Because attitudes cannot be hidden over a sustained period of time, overcoming gift-blockers is imperative to walking in your gift. They reflect you; they reflect your spirit. And we need to remember at all times that "it's God's Spirit in a person, the breath of the Almighty One that makes wise human insight possible. The experts have no corner on wisdom . . ." (Job 32:8 The Message).

> "You are responsible not only for what you do say
> but also for what you do not say."
> – Martin Luther

Love

Although we have discovered how powerful fear is, it is important to remember that love is much more powerful and our brains were made to operate in love. Each of us has our own familiar electrical chemical balance where we feel at peace. It's almost like a perfect idle rate that runs on the love attitude.[13]

Philippians 2:5 tells us, "You must have the same attitude Christ has" (LAB). This might seem impossible to do when we are operating in fear. The fact is that it is impossible because we cannot operate in both love and fear at the same time.

A love attitude is disrupted each time we create a new toxic thought or activate an existing toxic thought – a fear attitude, which is a gift-blocker. Any disruption in the body and mind's regular and consistent electrical chemical balance – love attitude – will result in discomfort, and we will consciously and unconsciously try to restore the balance.[14] It is important that you learn to identify this discomfort because it is a conscious and nonconscious mental activation of an attitude.

That's when you have the opportunity to examine that attitude to see whether it's a love or fear attitude. And if you continue to focus on fear, your gift will be blocked. Your brain and body will respond automatically and distort the love circuit into the fear circuit.

> The meaning of things lies not in the things themselves, but in our attitudes toward them.

Even though fear is powerful, operating in love is even more powerful, and fear is a gift-blocker. You can choose. Even though you may not be able to choose your circumstance, you have the choice to operate in fear or love.

14

CHAPTER FOURTEEN: {DISCOMFORT ZONES}

In the last chapter, we learned about the importance of recognizing discomfort when we are not operating in love. Now, let's explore this discomfort a little more deeply because it can grow into a toxic gift-blocker if it is not caught early.

There are two zones, where discomfort can indicate a possible gift-blocker:

- The "just aware" level
- The "adrenalin-pounding, heart-pumping" level

Both of these levels can easily be felt because of the discomfort caused by the interruption in the regular, consistent and comfortable level of our body's millions and millions of minute and complex electrical chemical reactions and transactions taking place at any one time.[15]

If we can train ourselves to identify these discomfort zones, we are on the way to dealing with gift-blocker(s) and being freed from the chains of toxicity and the fear attitudes they produce.

The easiest way to visualize this will be to reference the *Inside the Brain* diagram on page 69 which will show you these parts of the brain as I describe them.

We get input from the environment, our body and our thoughts. This information is then transmitted via a structure called the thalamus to the outer cortex of your brain where memories (thoughts) are stored.

This area of the brain looks like a big forest, because these thoughts look like trees.

The information flies through these "trees" – your memories/thoughts – alerting them to the new incoming information, much like the preview of a movie does. This is the first place where attitude is activated; it is literally "switched on" as the information sweeps through the memory trees like a breeze – "the breeze through the trees."

This is how your brain makes sense of new information; it references connections with previous experiences and memories. It may land on a memory that is similar, and if it's a good memory, you will experience a subtle warm and happy feeling, just outside of your conscious mind.

If, however, the memory is negative, feelings of turbulence will start and your peace will be disturbed. This is the first point where your attitude will start developing on a nonconscious level. You can't quite place it yet, but something is starting to happen in your brain. This is the "just-aware" level, the first zone.

What do we do at this zone to either deal with the toxic thought cluster, the gift-blocker, or prevent a gift-block from happening? We need to respond to this "just-aware" quickening. Never ignore it because it's alive, real and dynamic and will produce either healthy fruit or toxic fruit. Analyze this "quickening," this witness in you, and bring it into your conscious awareness. This is an anticipation built into you that is responding to knowledge. It is a fear or love anticipation building up in you.

This is important because it is the epigenetic (over and above the genetic expression of something) level, meaning there is an environment developing outside of the new memory about to be built that is going to influence exactly what and how the memory is going to look and feel – healthy or toxic. Our minds affect which genes in our neurons are expressed.[16]

Genetic expression happens when a memory is built. Our brains are designed to respond to knowledge, and you need to detect whether this information is good or bad for you. This "just-aware preview" of the information will influence how you feel about the information, but it's very subtle, not quite a conscious thought yet.

The "just-aware" zone has the purpose of protecting and guarding your mind because, quite simply, "toxic in, toxic out." What does this mean for us? It means that if the incoming knowledge and thoughts are good and based on love, your gift and wisdom will be further developed. But if information is negative and fear-based, chemicals that disrupt thinking are released into the brain, producing stress, and manifest in some way – through worry or another gift-blocker.

We need to remember that every thought has an emotional component attached to it, a "chemical signature." These peptides, chemicals that are released, come from part of the brain I call the chemical factory – the hypothalamus found deep in the middle of your brain.

The hypothalamus has a host of "recipes" for attitude made up of the "chemical signature" of the thoughts and the attached emotion. It uses the peptides (small proteins that are chemical messengers made in the hypothalamus and released by the pituitary) to make a chemical signature for each attitude.[17] The hypothalamus translates the attitude into a physical reality in the body via the neurochemicals. If the attitude is love-based this is great; but if it is toxic it will cascade the body into chemical chaos.

So "catching" the possible growth of a toxic thought is the best way to prevent a gift-blocker from being planted and taking hold.

The "Adrenalin-Pumping, Heart-Pounding" Level

What happens when a toxic thought takes root and does grow? After the "just aware" zone and the chemicals start flowing, your attitude is about to develop into the "adrenalin-pumpin, heart-pounding" level.

These little chemicals are called "molecules of emotion and information," and they carry the emotions you are feeling, all the way into another part of your brain, just below the chemical factory.

This is the library of the brain holding emotional perceptions. Its "brain" name is the amygdala (don't worry, you don't have to remember these names), and it's about the size of an almond. The amygdala works very closely with the hypothalamus, which monitors the flow of chemicals and attitudes.

Even here we see uniqueness in each one of us because we each have our own balance; our own individual internal chemistry is affected by nature, nurture and most importantly, our own unique way of thinking, our gift. We can enhance or upset our own balanced state just by our thoughts. Isn't that amazing?

Once the electrochemical signature that is activated by a thought in the outer part of the brain hits this library of emotional perceptions, you may *feel* a strong physical reaction: stress chemicals start flowing, which makes your heart pump faster; adrenalin flows and you feel that rush that almost jerks you off your feet; cortisol flows blocking your memory for a few moments; your muscles tense; your breathing becomes shallow and rapid.

It is almost unbelievable, but you will have more than 1400 known physical and chemical reactions and more than 30 different neurotransmitters and hormones activated – this is stress. If you stay in this state of stress for too long, nerve cells and memory will die off. These chemicals can set off a cascade of destructive reactions inside a nerve cell, sometimes even causing "cell suicide." These will manifest as gift-blockers like anxiety, depression or illness (see an image of the Fear Tree on page 145).[18]

But remember, God has given provision in everything. He has given us a way to handle this "adrenalin-pumping, heart-pounding" level.

When you feel stress that does not dissolve quickly, it is strong evidence that you have a gift-blocker – or maybe several – in action. This emotional perceptual library (the amygdala) does not always provide the truth, because it works on perceptions, and perceptions are sometimes false. In fact a lot of the time the emotions in this amygdala library are quite dangerous if you follow them or allow them to control you.

So, what should you do to move out of this state of stress?

You can take advantage of a circuit God has built into your brain that runs between the amygdala and the front part of the brain called the prefrontal cortex (PFC), which is situated more or less behind your eyebrows.

Operating much like a scale, this circuit helps to balance reason and emotion. This is because the frontal lobe, of which the PFC is a part, is directly connected to all the other parts of the brain and therefore holds the power. The PFC also has at its command the basal forebrain that activates all the processing loops through the brain.[19] It manages and coordinates and integrates all other brain regions.

The PFC, helps us reason and understand our own thoughts about ourselves. We use this PFC-amygdala circuit to control the raging emotion and stress response in our body. This is part of the love circuit described earlier. We do this by reasoning out the situation facing us in our minds or out loud – almost as though we are standing outside of ourselves thinking about our thinking. Our frontal lobe is really great at this. If we don't do this we will fall prey to the fear circuit described earlier. If we do control the fear, the corpus striatum is activated (discussed earlier) which makes us feel calm, peaceful and confident.

Acknowledging feelings is of paramount importance because the emotions, as I have explained, are dynamic chemicals that flow in the bloodstream between cells depositing information about the memory into cells! If you suppress an emotion – it will explode somewhere.

You can restore balance by observing your own thinking and making decisions about your thoughts and emotions. You can acknowledge any toxic feelings and then make a decision whether you will live in them or release them. Toxic feelings don't have to be a permanent part of your thoughts.

Emotions Do not Have Control
As we reviewed earlier, you do not have to let emotions control you.

Even the painful toxic ones – or any toxic feelings for that matter, toxic feelings you have been nursing for so long and are so familiar to you that you think they are "normal." You can analyze them and because of the neuroplasticity of the brain, rewire them.

For example, you may have been abused as a child and find that emotions are awakened each time you move into a new relationship, affecting the new relationship negatively. Another example is you may have been scared of math for years, and as soon as you walk into the math class, emotions of anxiety and fear well up in you, resulting in a negative attitude. This will block your ability to take in any information during the lesson.

It is really important that you deal with the emotion activated or it will control you. Therefore, in dealing with this "adrenalin-pumping, heart-pounding" level of attitude, acknowledge and analyze the strong emotion you are feeling. God has given you a very powerful frontal lobe to do this.

Don't react to it; think first and if possible, put it "back on the shelf" and tell yourself something positive like, "I don't like math because I think I am not so good at it, but I am going to conquer this fear, face it and ask questions till I do understand." And if it doesn't work the first time, do it again and again and again.

Science tells us that you need to practice using something or studying something at least seven times in repeated intervals over time before you are going to be able to use the information or perform the skill.[20]

Getting your attitudes under control normally takes about 21 days, and the first four are the hardest, so don't give up! Like anything that is a process, the results are well worth the effort. Eventually you will be able to use this amazing circuit that is built into the love circuit of the brain to balance reason and emotion. When you do that, you have taken a giant leap in the direction of bringing all your thoughts into captivity (2 Corinthians 10:5) and renewing your mind (Romans 12:2).

It may sound daunting to try capturing all of your thoughts. But when you understand how you can scientifically choose what becomes part of who you are, you will also understand that you have an amazing opportunity. We all have the opportunity to choose to walk in the gift God has given us – despite circumstances.

15

CHAPTER FIFTEEN:
{YOU *CAN* CHOOSE – THE SCIENTIFIC PROOF}

It is remarkable that the information we grow onto nerve cells in our brains, the trees of our mind will bring healing or destruction. We understand the importance of the Tree of Life and the Tree of Knowledge and of good and evil from the Bible. Well, in science, we can look at nerve cells, which also have roots and are much the same structurally.

Have a look at the tree images in chapter 13 to see what I am talking about, and as you do, think about this Scripture, one of my favorites (I even put it on my business card)" . . . down the middle of the great street of the city. On each side of the river stood the tree of life, bearing twelve crops of fruit, yielding its fruit every month. And the leaves of the tree are for the healing of the nations" (Revelation 22:2 NIV).

Although the parallels between science and Scripture are remarkable, the most amazing thing is, *you* can choose whether you would like to grow a healthy "love attitude" tree that brings health and life into your brain or a toxic thorny "fear attitude" tree that will bring death into your brain (see Love Tree and Fear Tree on pages 144-145).

It all has to do with your gift and the I-factor.

I am going to show you this truth from a scientific perspective in this chapter, so you can confidently know that with God's help, you have the ability to make good decisions and reject the world's philosophy of the gene myth that tells us human freedom is but a delusion and genes control all. Your genes are not an unalterable blueprint or a life sentence. DNA is not your destiny.[21]

We are not victims of our biology; rather God has designed us in such a way that biology works for us. He has endowed us with the ability to be self-reflective, and the self-conscious mind is extremely powerful. We have the incredible capacity to override conscious and nonconscious memories – both toxic and non-toxic – and actively choose how to respond or not respond to environmental signals and internal signals from your thought life.

God calls us daily to make use of this gift of choice He has given us, "I call Heaven and Earth to witness against you today: I place before you Life and Death, Blessing and Curse. Choose life so that you and your children will live" (Deuteronomy 30:19 The Message).

In my practice, I always made a point of focusing on the gift of my patients as I mostly saw children and teenagers and adults who had given up all hope in their ability to learn and achieve anything in life. My greatest joy was seeing a patient walk out of my practice with hope in their eyes and the message in their hearts that it is a scientific fact that they have an amazing brain they can develop and that they are gifted.

Some of my favorite experiences were receiving text messages from formerly-rebellious teenagers who originally only came to see me because their parents were at their wits' end when it came to dealing with them, but at the end of our time together, considered me a friend. I remember one young man who sent me a text, "Dr. Leaf, you have changed my life; I have hope again."

Probably one of my favorite stories of hope comes out of my time working in South Africa among the poorest of schools and my goal was to try to help 12th graders pass their exams. The conditions were abysmal with no decent facilities – one textbook among 100 children and a chalkboard that didn't work. And many of these children hadn't eaten for days at a time.

One particular young man always stands out in my mind, because when I arrived in his classroom he was angry with life, hungry and tired and weighed down with the burdens of having sickness in his home, living in extreme poverty and a whole host of other toxic things in his life that I didn't know about.

I remember him glaring at me as I got up to teach him and his classmates how to learn. I remember thinking that this young man had no hope, just pain, and I asked God to help me touch his heart.

Well, at the end of a long six-hour day, the teachers asked who wanted to thank me. Holding up a pen, this young man rushed to the front, tears pouring from his eyes, and said to me, "Dr. Leaf, thank you, thank you. Now I know what to do with my pen."

This was one of those defining moments in my life, and I vowed to get this message of hope to as many hopeless people as I could, because the message of the brain is a message about our Creator. That young man found God that day, and his face will always be in my mind.

I treasure these memories and am blessed to have many. The change I see in the people in these memories inspired me to study more about the brain so I can have a deeper understanding of how great God has made us.

This message of the gift and healing of toxic thoughts and "gift-blockers," that the brain can change and anyone can learn, is so liberating and filled with hope. It will always be the mission of my heart to build this hope into people because it is truth.

As Scripture says, "Hope deferred makes the heart sick, but a longing fulfilled is a tree of life" (Proverbs 13:12 NIV).

I want to stimulate a hope and longing in you to find and develop and use your gift. I want you to be so filled with hope and love that you will pour this into someone else who, in turn, will pour into someone else. I want this gift message of hope to go viral!

Now, let me show you from a scientific perspective that choice has mental "real-estate" and that we *can* choose between the tree of life and the tree of death. We also need to see the consequences or fruit of these choices.

If you recall, in the previous chapter I told you about the "adrenalin-pumping, heart-pounding" level where you can identify a gift-blocker; now I am going to tell you about what comes after this. I love to call it the "about-to-make-a-decision" level. This is where we deal with choice, and it all happens around the front of the brain, the frontal lobe.

I think God's grace was lavish when He made this part of the brain because it does so much and gives us so much independence that we can almost become proud at our own intellectual capacity. But having said this, we must always remember, it is only in the voluntary self-surrender to God that we will truly release that gifts inside of us. If not, God says, "I will destroy the wisdom of the wise and discard the intelligence of the intelligent" (1Corinthians 1:19 LAB).

The frontal lobe (also call the prefrontal cortex) is capable of an impressive display of functions, is connected to all other parts of the brain, and is where all the neural connections converge. It also houses the brain's most sophisticated circuits. This enables the frontal lobe to integrate and manage all the activities of all other parts of the brain.

When the frontal lobes move into high gear, they understand and observe our own thoughts about ourselves and make decisions about those thoughts. Your ability to choose and all the skills required to prepare for decision-making are situated behind your eyes to about halfway across your head.[22] The frontal lobe moves into extreme high activity when something is novel and when a decision to build a thought or new memory is about to happen. This ability to think about what you are thinking about is necessary to make a decision.[23]

Information swirls through the middle of the brain in a tube called the hippocampus around an area called the corpus callosum. As the information moves toward the frontal lobe, it becomes amplified and highly active, and expectancy (hope) builds, which is expressed through various neurotransmitters. This active "thinking-about-thinking" is sharpened when we are operating in our gift. Neurotransmitters (chemicals that carry the messages) are released into the area where the memory is going to be built, creating a healthy love environment within which the memory is built.

The neurotransmitters activate proteins to be released inside the cell, turning on a "switch" gene, the creb gene, which acts like a light switch that *we choose* to switch on by our thoughts. The creb gene then activates genetic expression and proteins to build the memory are made.

When we choose to switch on the creb gene because of the thoughts we allow to permeate our brain, protein synthesis happens and a branch grows making a new synaptic connection between the axon (long part like a tree trunk) of one nerve cell and the dendrites (branched part, looks like the top of a tree) of the adjacent cell (see diagram on page 32).[2]

A temporary memory is born. Then we have to think about that information repeatedly over time to cause another permanent type of building protein to form, which will change the temporary memory into a permanent memory (thought).

But if we don't focus on it, the temporary memory will disappear after about 48 hours.[25] So it's pretty much up to us whether we will build memory which will become part of us or not.

God has given us the frontal lobe to evaluate the information we want to build into permanent memory. Still, nothing happens until we think hard enough about the information to cause the cascade of proteins and chemicals to do their work, and even then, once this has happened, we have to switch that gene on to actually grow the memory. All the way through the thought process we have a choice.

Science and Scripture make us look in the mirror of
personal responsibility.

In fact, God has designed the brain in such a way that as a memory is brought out of the nonconscious mind into the conscious mind it becomes unstable and has to change – either in a more toxic or less toxic direction: it never stays the same. That's great news for us because we can fix – rewire – toxic memories. Your amazing ability to use your frontal lobes to stand outside of yourself and observe your own thinking provides the fuel for this change.[26]

This is great news and is basically the scientific way of saying we can renew our minds (Romans 12:2). Once again, we have a scientific principle catching up with a biblical principle.

What this means is that once a memory has moved from the nonconscious into the conscious, it never goes back the same way – it will either go back worse (more toxic) or it will go back better (less toxic or toxic-free). The point being, the memory, once conscious, will never be the same again. It will change in some way. This is the confirmation we *can* change toxic thoughts that are gift-blockers. For instance, this is how people who have suffered trauma can alter the unpleasant memory.

Old memories or existing thoughts will be dealt with in pretty much the same way: They get awakened from the nonconscious and brought into consciousness, evaluated by the frontal lobe and then changed in some way. And *you* are the epigenetic force in this whole equation. It's your thoughts that get this whole thing going. If you have gift-blockers activated, then you can lose information because it won't be built into your thought clusters properly.

Gift-blockers will also affect the clarity of your thought and your ability to use the frontal lobe in the way it should be working in this self-evaluative, decision-making, choice function. As toxic levels rise, meaning the gift-blockers are increasing, all the chemicals needed to build the memory, as well as the electrical chemical feedback loops that run the brain and body, will become distorted.

For example, earlier on I spoke about how toxic thoughts can increase the level of glutamate, which, in the right quantities, is very important to memory building, but in the wrong quantities, it acts like battery acid, causing damage in the brain. Where there is damage, there will be inflammation, and all this combined starts affecting the function of nerve cells in that particular area. This may manifest in various problems, such as depression or anxiety or learning problems or physical health issues and so on (see Fear Tree on page 145).

Let's look a little closer at the trees we can choose between in the next chapter.

16

CHAPTER SIXTEEN:
{YOU CAN CHOOSE THE LOVE TREE
OR THE FEAR TREE}

Up until now we have been talking about our gifts as the unique way we think. You have worked through the profile to find and interpret your gift, and I have told you how you can recognize through your attitude that you have gift-blockers in action. I have also shown you from a scientific perspective that choice is a brain fact and you can choose your reactions to the situations and circumstances of life.

Now, I want to discuss the two trees we can choose to build in our life and their consequences. I want to show you the consequences of investing in your thought life in either the fear or love direction. It is also very important to recognize the depth of how our thoughts affect our brains and our biologies. Our thoughts are the roots, while the affects are the branches, fruits and leaves on the tree.

Our gifts – how we think – can select, modify and regulate gene activity. This means our genetic expression is constantly being remodeled in response to life experiences. Our perceptions of life shape our biology and the character of our lives.[27] Because you have a unique way of thinking that no one else has, you will filter information and see the world differently than anyone else.

Your gift operates best in a peaceful love, not fear, environment: "Then, because you belong to Christ Jesus, God will bless you with peace that no one can completely understand. And this peace will control the way you think and feel" (Philippians 4:7 CEV). So, thoughts are the mind's electrical chemical energy – or fuel – and they will directly influence how the brain controls the body and itself.

This thought energy can activate or inhibit the proteins cells make, so we can never avoid the fact that there will be consequences to how we invest in our thoughts. Our genes don't control our thoughts; our thoughts control our genes.[28]

If you choose to see a world filled with love and wonder and beauty, your brain and body will respond by growing in health. If, however, you choose to believe in a dark world filled with fear, your brain and body will become toxic and sick.

Trees have roots planted in soil, which provides the environment from which they obtain nourishment. In my image of the "Fear Tree," you will see twelve roots that are twelve areas of toxic thinking that flourish in fearful soil (see page 145).

These are gift-blockers. The implications of these are huge in that when you make a decision to change your life, you need to pay attention not only to the seeds that are being planted in your mind but what kind of soil is providing nourishment – love or fear.

For example, if you are coming out of an alcohol addiction, you should not mix with people drinking alcohol or frequent the places where you used to drink alcohol. If you do, you risk planting your thoughts back into fear soil and the old manifestation will try to grow back from this "nourishment." On the branches of this Fear Tree are the manifestations of fear – these have grown out of the trunk of stress, which is the result of each area of toxic thinking, as we have learned.

Out of the soil of fear grows the trunk of stress. And out of the trunk of stress grows, for example, the branches of anxiety, depression, addictions, physical illness and learning disorders. The fruits of these will be the different types of anxiety and depression and illness and so on. The roots produce fruit and, in the case of the "tree of fear and death," toxic fruit.

Through all the biological explanations given up till now, we see that our thoughts will have consequences, which are manifestations – the toxic fruit on the tree. 87-95% of mental and physical illness today comes from our thought lives – these illnesses are the bad fruit on the tree.[29]

Then there is the Love Tree whose roots are the opposite of the toxic roots – healthy thinking, healthy emotions, healthy words and other elements that nourish your gift. This tree grows in the soil of love, growing branches of forgiveness, caring, selflessness, truth, hope, trust, looking for the best, perseverance, faith (1 Corinthians 13), joy and peace, patience, kindness, gentleness, faithfulness and self-control (Galatians 5:22-23 NIV). These will manifest in the fruits of happiness and fun and calmness, allowing you to enjoy life and grow in your gift.

We are each so different, so no one description will cover all the different types of manifestations of our thought lives. The branches and fruits of the dirty dozen (the roots of the Fear Tree) are definitely not all-inclusive, but give a broad idea of the concept. As medical science and neuroscience progress and we get deeper understanding, we will discover even more.

Each of us will manifest the Fear Tree and the Love Tree in our own unique way, so what I have done in the next section is briefly explain the branches and fruits – the manifestations or consequences of the gift-blockers. In the following chapters I will talk about each one of these separately, so you can better understand how to uproot them and start walking in your gift!

PART FOUR: Overcoming Gift-Blockers

INTRODUCTION

You have an amazing gift, a unique and special way of thinking, so you see the world from a distinct perspective. As we go through life and interact with others, we use and develop our gifts. That's how God has designed us. However, the reality is that we have toxic thought clusters with their attached emotions that can affect how well we use our gifts and how effectively our gifts develop.

Unfortunately there *are* consequences to toxic thinking, especially where the efficiency of our gifts are concerned. When toxic seeds are planted these consequences grow into – "branches" (see image on page 145).

I have noticed from my experience and research that there appear to be five main "branches" that can grow out of toxic thinking. These include (but are not limited to):[1]

- physical manifestations, for example, cardiovascular problems, digestive problems, immune system disorders, skin disorders, to name just a few
- learning manifestations, for example, learning disorders, underachieving potential
- anxiety disorders, for example, phobias, obsessive-compulsive disorders, post traumatic stress disorders, panic attacks
- depressive disorders
- addictions (alcohol, pornography, worry, etc.)

If the soil is not nourishing and the root system isn't healthy, a tree can have a very difficult time thriving. In fact, it will struggle. Just like a tree, if our environment is toxic and if we have toxic thoughts and gift-blockers, it is difficult for us to thrive. It will be a struggle to operate how we were created to operate in our gifts.

There are twelve areas of toxic thinking in our lives that form the roots of the "Fear Tree" (see image of the Fear Tree on page 145).

Every time you have a thought, it actively changes your brain and your body – for better or for worse. There are twelve areas of toxic thoughts, which can be as harmful as poison to our minds and our bodies. Toxic thoughts don't just creep into our minds as a result of abuse or an especially horrific trauma, but they affect people in all stages of life, in every part of the world, every day. Even something as small as a minor irritation can become toxic and needs to be swept away.

Here are twelve areas where toxic thoughts can creep in and grow into gift-blockers (see page 145):[2]

- Toxic Thoughts
- Toxic Emotions
- Toxic Words
- Toxic Love/Faith
- Toxic Dreams
- Toxic Choices

- Toxic Touch
- Toxic Seriousness/Health/Schedules
- Toxic Unforgiveness/Faith

Just like any seed, when these toxic elements are planted, they grow. Toxic seeds often take root, growing into a tree with the expression of toxic thoughts and watered with fear. The twelve areas have been separated from each other to better explain them, but they will uniquely combine together according to the structure of your gift – the way you think about life.

I cannot recreate the exact routes for toxic thoughts (gift-blockers) you may be struggling with, nor can I say for sure what the outcome will be. But when you understand the concept, you will find hope in knowing you can overcome gift-blockers. That's why I share stories of real people who have gone through and are going through toxic thinking. These are profiles of real people, but names and details have been changed.

Never forget, you can choose to change. You can choose to live in love or in fear. You can choose to let habits direct your steps or to walk in your gift. There is no manifestation or fruit that is greater than your free-will. I have tried to show you this from science with the amazing neuroplasticity of the brain.

Tree of Fear

In the toxic soil watered by fear, your gift can become distorted – causing you to struggle to operate in your gift. In the soil of love, your gift will grow and mature.

Let's take Kim, for example, who has an eating disorder. Although there are many causes for an eating disorder, let's use Kim as an extreme example of someone who is struggling with one of the most powerful gift-blockers, rooted in fear. The way Kim receives information, her first pillar, will influence how something toxic takes root in her mind.

So for this example, let's assign Kim's top pillar as logical; this means she would receive information through logic and reasoning and rationalization.

Perhaps when Kim was a child, someone said something to her about her appearance, and she applied her own unique logic to the words. Kim came to her own "rational" toxic conclusion based on her perceptions, even if someone didn't mean for their words to be toxic. Her conclusion then became a toxic seed, taking root, growing and influencing her perception of herself, specifically her body image and her self-esteem – these toxic words turned into toxic thoughts.

These toxic thoughts generated toxic emotions because she felt bad about herself and what she looked like and made the incorrect assumption that everyone looked at her in the same way she looked at herself. As she meditated more and more on this, the thought cluster and negative attitude grew stronger. She chose not to discuss this with anyone, but instead internalized it, which added even more distorted perceptions to it.

As time went on the emotion grew, eventually turning into hatred for her own body, and toxic health was birthed. Over the years the toxic words and toxic seeds and toxic thoughts and toxic emotions manifested as increasing levels of depression in Kim, and an addiction was developing. Kim started making some toxic choices. By a certain age, a full-blown eating disorder had developed – depression and anxiety working with it.

Of course, not all toxic seeds grow into eating disorders; that example is an extreme one. Everyone will react differently because our gifts allow us to perceive the world differently. And obviously, one statement was not the cause of such an extreme example. Rather the toxic seed, nourished by fear, grew. Although the seed may not grow into something as visible or recognizable, healthy trees never grow from toxic seeds, and vice versa. The point is, gift-blockers are obstacles to walking in your gift.

But there is freedom from gift-blockers. As in all things, we are not meant to be bound by chains. Rather, we have been given freedom in the Lord. We have been given the opportunity to overcome circumstance – including gift-blockers that prevent us from living in the gifts we have been given.

CHAPTER SEVENTEEN:
{TOXIC THOUGHTS AS GIFT-BLOCKERS}

A thought may seem like something that is fleeting. A thought may seem harmless and of no consequence. Often, we think of actions as having more impact than thoughts but actions are generated from thoughts. So it is important to realize that thoughts are measurable and occupy mental "real estate."

Thoughts are active: They grow and change. Thoughts influence every decision, word, action and physical reaction we make. A thought may seem harmless. But if it becomes toxic, even just a simple thought can become physically, emotionally or spiritually dangerous.

What are "toxic thoughts" and how are they different from healthy thoughts? Toxic thoughts are thoughts that trigger negative and anxious emotions, which produce biochemicals that cause the body stress. They are stored in your mind, as well as in the cells of your body.

The surprising truth is that every single thought – whether positive or negative – goes through the same cycle when it forms. Thoughts are basically electrical impulses, chemicals and neurons on a physical level, but when put together, something amazing happens, something science is still attempting to explore and explain adequately – a unique thinking pattern emerges, different from every other person on the planet. This is very powerful because it means we have a distinct thinking signature – just as fingerprints are different and distinct to each person, so are our thought patterns, our gifts.

Thoughts look like a tree with branches. As the thoughts grow and become permanent, more branches grow and the connections become stronger (see diagram on page 32).

A thought becomes a gift-blocker when it is negative or toxic because the chemicals that it triggers simply block your ability to think clearly. For example, if you are worrying about something that has popped into your mind, the more attention you pay to the thought, the more it will grow and develop. It can cause you to worry, affecting your concentration during the day, your sleep at night, even making you feel ill in the process. This means the mind and body really are inherently linked, and this link starts with our thoughts.

So, what unique and distinct combination of thoughts is filling your mind today, and what is hidden in the depths of your nonconscious mind waiting to spring into consciousness and influence the choices you make? How many could-have, would-have, if-only thoughts are swirling through your head at this moment? What thoughts are consuming you? At what level of detail are you replaying things in your mind?

Life throws things at us that just seem to fill our brains with toxic thoughts, and they seem so hard to control. We all know this.

I have gone through many of those experiences that I would have preferred to not have on my resume of life, and I am sure you have as well. In hindsight I can always see God was working behind the scenes and that there was value to the lessons I learned. I have seen on every occasion how, when I indulged in self-pity or worry, the fruit turned bad, I felt the life draining out of me, while the gift-blocker gained strength.

I knew I had to "bring those thoughts into captivity," repent and forgive so peace and joy would flood my being again, freeing my gift. Then I would get lost in the joy of my family and my work once again.

Have you ever found yourself going to sleep thinking about a situation and then waking up thinking about the situation? Has your head ever been so filled with the toxic thought details of everything, it felt like you had to shake it to make some room for something else?

Have you ever had toxic thoughts consuming your every moment and coloring your attitude to everything?

If you have answered yes to any of the above, the chances are you have experienced toxic thinking and therefore have gift-blockers! Those toxic thoughts did nothing but harm your peace and block your ability to think clearly. You may even have lost your peace and sense of purpose in those moments.

Did you notice that as you stopped the cycle of toxic thinking, your gift started to operate again?

I know each time I indulge a gift-blocker, I can recognize a lack of peace and the "adrenalin-pumping, heart-pounding" I experience (see chapter 14).

Here are some typical emotionally-charged toxic thoughts which activate that discomfort level in the brain and those "adrenalin-pumping, heart-pounding" reactions:

- I can't do this.
- I am so stressed.
- I can't cope.

- I just know it won't work.
- I hate school.
- I hate my job.
- I am not artistic.
- I just don't have the energy to make a change.
- I should care about it now, but it'll wait until tomorrow.
- Nothing ever seems to go right for me.
- I will start my studies tomorrow.
- I will start my diet tomorrow.
- I am just not good at anything.
- I am at the end of my rope.
- If only I were smarter.
- Mondays are not good days for me.

When the gift-blocker of toxic thinking is in motion, it's likely to produce some kind of fruit or combination of fruit – addictions, anxieties, learning problems, physical illness, depression because of the mind-body link.

That's why we must break the toxic gift-blockers by:

1. Choosing to capture those thoughts by using the powerful frontal lobe God has given us to stand outside of ourselves and evaluate the thoughts and to apply Godly wisdom to manage them.
2. Using the discomfort zones to help identify these thoughts that are gifts-blockers.
3. Rewiring.
4. Choosing to operate not in fear, but rather in love, in the promises of the Lord.

It's important to recognize that there are several opportunities to break the toxic cycle and that we really can choose to operate in our gifts – despite our circumstance or our past.

Chapter Eighteen:
{TOXIC EMOTIONS AS GIFT-BLOCKERS}

Toxic emotions and toxic thoughts are intertwined and inseparable. This is because our thoughts have an emotional component associated with them. All thoughts are emotionally charged, so when you bring a thought up into consciousness, you also bring up the attached emotion.

When you think, you will also feel.

As we reviewed earlier, there are only two types of emotion – love and fear – and all other emotions stem from these, each derivative forming its own chemical "signature," meaning each thought has its own chemical "signature." The result is that our thinking quite literally becomes "feeling" with a resultant chemical reaction in our brains and bodies.

The problem of gift-blocking begins when thoughts and emotions become unbalanced and toxic. If feelings dominate, a neurochemical rush can start to distort feelings in the direction of fear, which can result in stress.

Furthermore, the brain is constantly changed by each encounter and interaction, the depth of impact is determined by our emotions.

If you don't control these toxic emotions they will surge. And the surge will turn into a flood. Once there is a flood, it is very difficult to stop – emotions will saturate, run wild and become addictive. If they are not controlled, these fear-distorted emotional signatures will start appearing on everything you think about, on every choice and in every behavior and every action. This will affect your ability to think with clarity and will block your gift.

Here's an example: your husband comes home from work and he has that look on his face that says, "not right now." But you have so much to tell him; you really want to discuss several matters.

When he lets you know that he needs time, through distance and facial expression, you are surprised by how abrupt he seems and you immediately think you have done something wrong or that something bad has happened. Now, your mind starts thinking of all the bad things that could go wrong, and each of these things that could go wrong has an emotion attached to it.

Within the ten minutes it takes your husband to settle down in front of the TV, you have thought of seven or eight different scenarios of what's wrong, and these and their attached emotions are swirling and stewing in your mind. So you approach your husband with eyes flashing and the floodgates open.

Your surprised husband, who was peacefully mulling over the day's events while flipping channels, looks up to find you blocking the TV screen, which you have planted your feet firmly in front of to get his full attention. Then you pour out your concerns and fears and ideas – each with its own chemical signature – and some concerns get thrown in that you think of as you are speaking while the tears just fall out your eyes and the words pour out your mouth.

Your husband brings his own set of chemical signatures to the event as he moves from surprise to irritation . . . you get the picture?

Emotions out of control will completely block your ability to "think things through." Submitting to them causes chemical chaos in the brain and makes your mind foggy. You lose concentration and will find it really difficult to listen to anything anyone is saying or trying to say to you. And this goes for all emotions.

Take a moment to think of a time when you let your emotions get out of control and try to remember how you felt when it happened.

The soil of fear fuels those distorted emotions wiping out any decent control from the frontal lobe, unless we make the choice to stop and bring balance back again. Going through life on an emotional rollercoaster is a gift-blocking disaster.

That's why we must break the gift-blocker of toxic emotions by:

1. Using the balancing circuit between the frontal lobe and the amygdala to balance reason and emotion.
2. Using the discomfort zones to help identify these gift-blocking emotions.
3. Capturing our thoughts (as in toxic thoughts above).
4. Never doing this without prayer and the help of the Holy Spirit.
5. Rewiring.

It's clear that we need to break the cycle of gift-blockers. Even though it may seem daunting to truly operate in your gift, to truly live out who you were created to be, you need to recognize that you have been given authority over gift-blockers.

You are not a victim to toxic situations or toxic seeds that can take root. You can learn to walk in your gift. And you can choose to walk in the confidence that your gift is intentional and purposeful. You were not made for anything less.

CHAPTER NINETEEN:
{TOXIC WORDS AS GIFT-BLOCKERS}

Are you paying attention to what words you are saying and what words you are receiving into your spirit?

Words reflect the thoughts and emotions of the speaker because every word was first a thought and an emotion. They are electro magnetic forces that cause real and lasting change both in the ears of the listener and you. And words really do cause pain. Researchers have shown that hurt feelings from words affect the same area in the brain – the cingulate gyrus – as a broken bone or physical injury. So the old Scottish nursery rhyme of "sticks and stones will break my bones but words will never harm me" is most certainly not true.[3]

Experts have also found that loving words help heal and rewire this pain. Words are the symbolic output of the exceptional processes happening on micro anatomical, epigenetic and genetic levels in the brain. They contain power to make or break you, your loved ones, your colleagues and your friends.

Are there words that have been spoken over you that have taken root and started blocking your gift? Perhaps you took an IQ test when you were younger and you were told you were average, but your brother or sister was above average. And this followed you into school and life. Or maybe you overheard someone say something about you, and you received that word into your spirit and made it part of you – the toxic words became toxic seeds.

When I think of these gift-blockers, I am reminded of Michelle.

Michelle had a rare medical condition that resulted in gaining weight. This condition took almost twelve years to sort out, which was an emotional rollercoaster for her. In the early years while the cause and solution were being sought, Michelle overheard her grandmother one day saying she was very overweight and that she was worried about her because she was gaining so much weight.

This threw Michelle off balance completely because she was so hurt by her grandmother's comments. She viewed them as a betrayal from someone she loved and trusted and who, instead of loving her, was watching every bite of food she took and constantly giving her funny looks which made her feel ugly and not unconditionally loved.

The intention of the granny was certainly not that; it was just concern handled poorly. But in the eyes and ears of a five-year-old, this was a catastrophe and changed the way she saw her grandmother and their relationship. Even today, that young lady who has now been healed and is slim and beautiful and healthy, still does not have a good relationship with her grandmother and she struggles with toxic seeds that were planted long ago.

Those toxic words and toxic looks spoke into that little girl's life and added a burden to her mind she didn't need to carry. As an adult, she could talk it through with someone who understands and who can help her rewire, but as a child, she did not even know how to express it.

Toxic words can change a life forever. But words can also heal. So it will be necessary for Michelle and her granny finally to sit down one day and talk this through. Those words which brought death to a relationship can be replaced with new words that can bring life to the same relationship.

Maybe you have had words spoken over your life that have wired a toxic pathway that is blocking your gift from truly operating. Maybe there are words that have not been spoken over you and the lack of kind, loving, affirming words has wired rejection or pain into your thought clusters blocking your gift.

That's why we must break the gift-blocker of toxic words by:

1. Using the discomfort zones to help identify and acknowledge gift-blocking toxic words that have been spoken over your life and that have taken root.
2. Using the discomfort zones to help identify and acknowledge gift-blocking toxic words that you are speaking over yourself and/or others.
3. Rewiring.
4. Never do this without prayer and the help of the Holy Spirit.

Although we can't be sure of the words that will be spoken over us in the future, we can choose to accept them as a part of who we are or not. We also can choose forgiveness and to walk in love, rather than fear which is the root of unforgiveness and bitterness.

CHAPTER TWENTY:
{TOXIC LOVE AS A GIFT-BLOCKER}

Early patterns of relating and attaching to others can get wired into our brains in childhood and repeated into adulthood. We saw this in the the previous chapter in the story of Michelle and her granny.

Our relationships are a product of our personal histories and experiences and are not biological instincts. We fall in love and make true friends with people not bodies.

As God looks on the heart and inward appearance (1 Samuel 16:7), we should remember that we are created in His image, despite the world's emphasis on biology and outward appearance.

Some biologists going down the evolutionary strand say we are attracted to certain people because they exhibit biological traits such as an hourglass figure (representing fertility) and muscles (the ability to protect). When we look at the outward appearance only, it is a distortion of how our brains are designed to form relationships, and the consequence is that people's abilities to form lasting relationships are affected – "I am not beautiful or thin enough to be loved." "I 'love' her or him because he or she looks a particular way." This is empty and misses all the deepness and beauty of real love.

We are not designed for toxic love. Distorted toxic love is learned fear and completely blocks our gifts. Healthy love on the other hand rewires the brain, increasing our health, intelligence and happiness. When our love circuit fires, it is more difficult for the learned fear to fire at the same time. When we move into Godly love, things don't bother us as much and we simply love being in love.[4]

Plasticity allows us to develop brains so unique from our responses to individual life experiences that it is sometimes hard to see the world as others do, to want what they want or to cooperate. It starts with making the choice to see people for who they really are; not to manipulate or be manipulated; to reach out to others in whatever way you can. As I have now said many times, choice is greater than any learned pattern of negative or selfish love. And as we *choose to change* to healthy love, dopamine and oxytocin increase and start melting down the old connections to prepare the way for the new ones.

Science is showing us that there is a massive unlearning of negative toxic thoughts when we operate in love. The brain releases a chemical called oxytocin, which literally melts away the negative toxic thought clusters so that rewiring of new non-toxic circuits can happen. This chemical also flows when we trust and bond and reach out to others. So love wipes out fear![5]

We also have another amazing chemical called dopamine that works with oxytocin. It flows as we expect and anticipate something and puts us on heightened alert to build new memories (as we imagine helping the person do well in a test, restore a relationship and so on) and gives us a thrilling surge of energy and excitement and confidence and motivation to carry on. And then as we actually help the person do well in the test, for example, endorphins are released that make us feel great. When we do good and reach out in love, God blesses us by helping our brains detox and increasing our motivation and wisdom thereby helping us negotiate life more successfully.[6]

That's why we must break the gift-blocker of toxic love by:

1. Using the discomfort zones to help identify and acknowledge gift-blocking toxic love.
2. Choosing to change.
3. Rewiring.
4. Never doing this without prayer and the help of the Holy Spirit.

Isn't it amazing that we have been given the opportunity to renew our minds when it comes to love? God is faithful in all things. So, even when it seems incredibly difficult to make new choices, know that lasting change really is possible!

21

CHAPTER TWENTY-ONE: {TOXIC DREAMS AS GIFT-BLOCKERS}

Dreams occur during REM (rapid eye movement) sleep. Changes in your brain are occurring in the neurons as memories consolidate, and across the brain as the thoughts integrate into the network. So essentially, the brain is sorting thoughts.

As you think in your own unique way, you will also dream in your own unique way, which means there are no predictable patterns. With God's help, however, sometimes you can better understand your "gift-blockers" from your dreams. All people dream, but not everyone always remembers his or her dreams.

This is because as you sleep your brain sorts out toxic and nontoxic thoughts in your dreams. Toxic thought clusters disturb the nerve chemistry and electrical-chemical feedback loops of the brain and body, disturbing peace and causing you to "forget" your dreams. I stress however, that no one except you and God can get meaning from your dreams because of the distinctiveness of how you think – your gift.

The process of how we dream is fascinating. We start with NREM sleep where the brain stops processing the outside world and progresses into REM sleep where we process our inner thought life. As we do this, we move through toxic and non-toxic thought clusters with all their associated emotions.[7] Dreams involve thinking about abstract ideas that are represented visually, so they can be confusing.

Neurochemically, when we are awake we have serotonin and norepinephrine helping us to line up our thoughts and think logically to process the sensory input coming from the outside world. Then we get bursts of acetylcholine as something captures our attention.[8]

At night-time when we sleep, acetylcholine is active (consolidating memories) and serotonin and norepinephrine shut down. It's the firing of acetycholine that brings the "strangeness" to our dreams.[9] Dreams start when a host of signals fires upwards from the pons (part of the brain stem) into the cortex activating memories, but not activating the fontal lobe's ability to understand the memories so there is no reasonable or rational explanation of the mix of memories activated. It appears the really intense memories, the very toxic and very happy memories get a lot of attention in this process.[10] As the signals move down to the emotional areas, the amygdala wakes up the emotional perceptions stored there, creating a busy dream characterized by feelings. The more toxic the thought clusters, the more frightening and anxiety-provoking the dreams become.

Dreams have purpose: Dreams are there to sort our thinking. And when they are recurring this could be an indication of a toxic thought that has not been resolved. Very often we dream issues that haven't yet been resolved, meaning there is something that is not sorted out in your thought life and needs to be faced so it can be rewired.

After studying brain scans, some dream experts suggest that perceptions are processed in dreams in a backward way, that we don't use our higher mental functions in the same way as when we are awake. We don't "see" things in quite the same way when we are asleep as we do during the day. These scans show that the areas dealing with emotion, relationships and survival (amygdala) and pleasure seeking (ventral tegmental area) are very active, but the frontal lobe that reasons, achieves goals, disciplines and controls behavior is less active.[11] This means we process from concrete to abstract during the day and abstract to concrete during the night.

You may have heard it is better to never let the sun set on your anger (Ephesians 4:26). Brain science demonstrates that it's true.

If you are upset with someone and go to bed angry, it is actually not helpful because you will consolidate that memory into your networks and because it's toxic, it will manifest at some point as a dream. The anger will often come out as part of a storyline of a book you have read or a movie you have seen, but backward because of perceptions being processed in a backward direction in dreams.[12]

Someone with a very rebellious spirit may have recurring dreams of breaking boundaries and could be represented visually by "I am flying" or other types of boundary-breaking dreams. Or someone may fear his or her ambition is out of control and have dreams of nation conquering.[13]

An example of this is a recurring dream I have been having for years until I learned that I could start to rewire it. I kept having a dream of someone breaking into my childhood home. It was the same root of fear but three different scenarios, and each time there was a nerve-wracking race to get out of the house away from the attacker or get into the house because the attacker is coming up the driveway or I am lying by a glass sliding door and I can hear the attacker. They were horrific and frightening and I would wake up in a cold sweat each time.

I spoke to my mother about them and apparently when I was very young our house was broken into and I saw the intruders from my window going around the house. It was traumatic for me as I was a young child.

Even now as an adult, I still get traumatized when I recall the dreams. They are much less frequent now, and when I have that dream I know that I need to continue working on rewiring that fear circuit. Because

I have this reoccurring toxic dream, I have a toxic fear that is difficult to get rid of.

This is an indirect gift-blocker because it shows me there is a cluster of thoughts with fear emotions intertwined within them that I haven't fully dealt with. This will cause a nagging stress and a nagging anxiety. Any kind of undealt with trauma will manifest in dreams in recurring ways. But as I continue to recognize it as fear, I also know that God has given me the opportunity to break free. Sometimes, this is more of a process than others. So, I see great progress and know that one day these dreams will stop completely.

Toxic dreams don't just come from frightening or negative experiences. If you have watched a particularly disturbing movie or heard a disturbing story, very often this will come out in dreams.

Once again, remember, you have a gift that operates when you are awake and asleep. Your unique way of sorting out your thought life in dreams will be your own unique experience, one worth investigating to try to sort out any disturbances to your mind's peace.

That's why we must break the gift-blocker of toxic dreams by:

1. Observing and journaling your dreams to increase awareness.
2. Prayerfully asking for the help of the Holy Spirit to tell you what they mean.

Toxic dreams can be harmful to a peaceful sleep. But they are useful in understanding that there may be "hidden" gift-blockers that need to be addressed. When you identify a gift-blocker, be assured that you can overcome it; you can walk in your gift confidently into lasting change.

CHAPTER TWENTY-TWO: {TOXIC CHOICES AS GIFT-BLOCKERS}

Before the end of today, you will have made many choices from the mundane (what to eat, where to sit, what to wear) to the more serious (what to do about a problem, an issue, a sickness, a child or friend problem, finances, what to do about your life). Choices we make are determined by our thoughts. So the healthier and more submitted our thoughts are to Christ, the healthier our choices. The converse applies as well. The more toxic our thought clusters and attitudes, the more toxic the choices we will make.

No choice stands in isolation. The choice you make was first a cluster of thoughts with its emotions attached, all forming your attitude. Your attitude is your state of mind that influences your choices. A general attitude – you are a negative or positive person; you tend to look on the bright side or dark side of life; you see the best or worst in people first; you first look at what went wrong before you look at what's right and vice versa; you see the cup half full or half empty, and so on. In addition to this general attitude are the individual emotions – attitudes – attached to each of your thought clusters; so you can have a good attitude about math but a bad attitude about history; you can have a good attitude to this person but a bad attitude to that person; you can have a good attitude in one situation and a bad attitude in another.

The bottom line of choices is this: When you walk in the structure of the gift that God has given you according to His will for your life, you are going to make healthy choices. We can identify if we are walking in love or fear by checking our activated thoughts and listening to that "adrenalin-pumping, heart-pounding" reaction we have to toxic thinking. Are you choosing toxic choices over healthy choices? Toxic choices can linger in our minds and our lives, causing us to experience emotions like regret, doubt and especially unforgiveness.

Twelve years ago I had to make a choice, one of the hardest I have ever had to make: whether to stay married.

My husband, Mac, was becoming an alcoholic. He had all kinds of toxic seeds from his childhood, which were manifesting in this toxic consequence. My love for him was so all-consuming that I felt I could not live without him; but one day, after he had driven me and our four children (ranging from three weeks up to five years old), back from a dinner drunk and would not let me drive, I realized I had reached the point of having to make a serious choice. I wrestled with God all night long. I knew I had to trust God.

I pleaded with God to heal him (Mac had been born again a couple of weeks before), telling God I could not live without him and I could help him give up drinking, that he was a great husband when sober and he never hurt us. But I knew God was telling me to let him go and trust Him – whatever that meant. And I knew I had been praying for him for nine years and had four small children.

The next morning when Mac woke up, I made the choice to trust God and, shaking, gave him a letter explaining that I was letting go and giving him to God. In that moment of truth I really thought I would die, because although deep down I knew he would do the right thing, there was still the question: What if he didn't?

Mac looked at me with tears in his eyes and said he would choose God and us over the bottle. He went inside the house and poured thousands of dollars of alcohol down the drain. He stopped drinking that day and has never touched another drink since.

He filled his bar in our home with spiritual food – Christian tapes and DVDs and CDs of worship music and Bibles and every book he could find about walking the Christian life. Today he runs our organization, and without him and his spiritual covering and love and support, I could not do what I do. He made the healthy choice to sell out to Christ and is the model husband and father, immersing himself in God and the Word. I am so thankful I chose to trust God that day and so thankful beyond words that Mac made the choice he did.

I am sure you have a story to tell about choices you have made. Maybe you have a similar or different story to mine. Maybe you made a toxic choice but now you want to make the right choice. Be heartened; God forgives and He blessed you with a brain that He can rewire, modeled after His own, to help you make the right choices.

That's why we must break the gift-blocker of toxic choices by:

1. Using the discomfort zones to help identify and acknowledge gift-blocking toxic love.
2. Using the frontal lobe to stand outside of ourselves and evaluate our choices and the thoughts and emotions they come from.
3. Rewiring.
4. Never doing this without prayer and the help of the Holy Spirit.

Sometimes in the middle of difficult circumstances, it is easy to forget that we have been given a choice. But we have! You have been given a choice about what steps you are going to take. And, when you are not bound by toxic choices, you can walk steadfastly in the gifting God has given you.

23

CHAPTER TWENTY-THREE: {TOXIC TOUCH AS A GIFT-BLOCKER}

Touch is lyrically described as "one of the most essential elements of human development," a "critical component of the health and growth of infants" and a "powerful healing force."

In studies by the late Wisconsin University psychologist Harry Harlow in the 1950s and 1960s, it is the force that cured baby rhesus monkeys of signs of stress, trauma and depression. Baby monkeys were removed from their mothers and suffered greatly. They were fed. They were cared for in every way, except for touch – especially the touch of their mothers. Pretty soon, the devastating affects became clear. They were withdrawn. They were listless. And they were not developing normally. However, when they were restored to their mothers' loving care, they became new creatures. They were curious. They were playful. And they were at peace.

Scientists are still discovering how very important touch is. Jesus, 2000 years ago, touched those He healed when He walked the earth; He held and loved and comforted through touch. A human connection is one of the most important elements in living in community with one another. However, toxic touch turns what is supposed to be a healing and healthy human connection into an ugly area of gift-blocking.

When something as basic as the need for touch – a great hug, a pat on the back, a peck on the cheek – turns into something toxic, toxic seeds and emotions and thoughts will all become part of the reaction.

We all know the stories. There are so many, it's overwhelming how the evil one has distorted touch in the world today. We know how hurtful abuse can be, when touch is harmful. And that is never, ever acceptable. But sometimes we don't realize that another aspect of toxic touch is actually the lack of touch.

In fact, just as inappropriate touch affects our gift, the lack of touch (called "cutaneous deprivation") will also affect our gifts through toxic emotions, thoughts and choices. Even physical growth and the immune system are weakened. Research shows that touch-deprivation causes change in the brain (neuroplasticity), laying the patterns for aggression and violence.[14]

There is a hunger more powerful than for food inside of us, we are wired by a loving God for loving touch. So that gentle pat on the hands or the kind tap on the back or the welcoming hug you gave someone today may very well have unblocked a toxic cycle in the brain and helped to release the person's gift. We are instrumental in helping heal each other through something as simple as loving touch. In fact, your touch could shift that person's day from a disaster to a success.

I know the joy and peace that I feel when Mac gives me a hug of encouragement when I have been sitting at my computer working hours on end on a new book or a new research project. And when I am feeling down, how a hug from one of my children can lift my spirit. And what about your pet? We have the cutest Shitzu who loves to lick – she will come up to you and in joy lick your feet until you laugh and pick her up to love her. This alone releases a neurochemical bath that not only relieves tension but activates your gift as well.

Those around you will benefit from the touch as well. Neuroscientists have discovered a very interesting function that neurons play when it comes to human interaction.

We have these amazing groups of neurons in the top and side of the brain (premotor cortex and inferior parietal cortex) that get excited and start firing the brain of the person receiving the hug. In fact the mirror neuron firing also happens in the person who made the decision to hug the other person as they identified with their issue and reached out in love.

We are designed for relationships – man is not meant to be alone, so it would make sense to have brain wiring to support healthy relationships. This is also why we love to hear other peoples' stories – the mirror neurons help make this real for us and we learn from each other.[15]

We each have our own natural inner pharmacy that produces all the drugs we ever need to run our body-mind in precisely the way it was designed to run. Of course, prescription drugs have their place. They can save lives. However, they are only a means to an end, and they usually have serious side effects. Good touching, on the other hand, releases the body's natural chemicals like endorphins, enkephalins, oxytocin and dopamine, setting in motion your love circuits and stopping the fear circuits.

Many animal and human studies show the benefits of touch, not only for depression, but for illnesses that have physical symptoms as well. So, missing, exaggerated, muted or otherwise distorted perceptions and responses become toxic thoughts, and thus affectionate touch is an essential "nutrient" to normal brain functioning.

That's why we must break the gift-blocker of toxic touch by:

1. Using the discomfort zones to help identify and acknowledge gift-blocking toxic touch . . . is it inappropriate or lacking?
2. Using the frontal lobe to stand outside of ourselves and evaluate how this can be changed.

3. Rewiring.
4. Never doing this without prayer and the help of the Holy Spirit.

So healthy touch is one of the physical things you can do to change your mental processes and unblock your gift.

24

CHAPTER TWENTY-FOUR: {TOXIC SERIOUSNESS AS A GIFT-BLOCKER}

Toxic seriousness encompasses toxic schedules and toxic health, and I have put these all together in one chapter because they work hand-in-hand. If we work too hard we won't take proper breaks to have some fun and we will most likely make toxic choices about what to eat and whether to exercise.

Sometimes we get so caught up in the cycle of toxic thoughts and emotions and words and choices that we forget who we are – our true selves – and we seem to operate like automatons doing what we are supposed to do and barely surviving.

God came to give us life and life more abundantly, but when we are toxic and not walking in our gifts, this pours out into our outlook and can be reflected in our schedules, the way we manage time and the choices we make about our health. Our bodies are amazingly resistant and can be pushed to extremes. But at some point your body and your brain will say "enough."

We can become too serious, but having fun is more infectious than a virus. In fact, it is viral. Try to not laugh when those around you are in paroxysms of hysterical laughter. Try having a bad day when you have just had a good belly laugh.

In fact, having fun will detox your gift-blockers, improve your health and make you clever to boot because your gift is neurologically developed when you have fun. Having fun is one of the most powerful antidotes to stress you will ever find. And it's free. It's a tremendous resource God has built into your brain to bring perspective into your life, help surmount problems, add sizzle to your relationships and make you feel good.

I love having fun with my children. They do the craziest things and say the funniest things that make me laugh. I love going for walks with them and the dogs and hearing their stories. I love sitting in the jacuzzi with them and making up silly songs and voices and – well, anything that makes us laugh. Our eldest daughter loves finding funny quotes that make us laugh. And Mac loves telling jokes. Our second daughter has a way of making comments that has us rolling, so we all wait in anticipation. Our son is always playing with words in a really funny way. If we allowed our schedules to take over, we never would have these important moments.

The point is, we cannot afford to be too serious because it will contribute to the breakdown of our gifts.

Many studies show why laughter deserves to be known as "the best medicine" (Proverbs 17:22). It releases an instant flood of feel-good chemicals that boost the immune system. Almost instantly, it reduces levels of stress hormones. A really good belly laugh can make cortisol drop by 39%, adrenalin by 70% and the "feel-good hormone," endorphin, increase by 29%. It can even make growth hormones skyrocket by 87%! Other research shows how laughter boosts your immune system by increasing levels of immunity and disease-fighting cells.[16]

Just look at some of the myriad of benefits of having fun; humor gets both sides of your brain working together, which is one of the keys to releasing potential. Some studies even suggest that laughter helps to increase the flexibility of thought and is as effective as aerobic exercise in boosting health in body and mind.

In fact, according to research, laughing 100 to 200 times a day is equal to 10 minutes of rowing or jogging! This sounds more fun than the gym!

Laughter quite literally dissolves distressing toxic emotions because you can't feel mad or sad when you laugh. When you laugh and have fun, endorphins are released which make you feel so great and at peace, those toxic thoughts can't get out of your brain fast enough. Fun protects your heart because when you laugh and enjoy yourself, your body releases chemicals that improve the function of blood vessels and increase blood flow, protecting against heart attack. Fun reduces damaging stress chemicals quickly, which, if they hang around in your body for too long, will make you mentally and physically sick. Fun and laughter also increase your energy levels.[17]

Wow . . . can you afford not to laugh?

Having fun through play and laughter is the cheapest, easiest and most effective way to control toxic thoughts and emotions and their toxic stress reactions. It rejuvenates the mind, body and spirit and gets positive emotions flowing.

And while you are having fun why don't you throw in an exercise routine to help boost your gift?

Exercise gets the heart to pump faster and more efficiently. Increased blood flow nourishes and cleanses the brain and organs, supplying the brain with much-needed oxygen and making you feel mentally sharper because you will cycle through your gift, your unique pattern of thought more efficiently. We need blood with oxygen to think, and we need the waste products of metabolism removed to think clearly and build memory and function properly. Exercise helps with this. If you break into a sweat, you will also get the added benefit of mood improvement prompted by the release of endorphins.

Exercise helps generate new brain cells. And stimulates the production and release of BDNF (neuronal growth factor) which plays a really important role in changing thinking.[18]

There are many different types of aerobic exercise, from running to cycling. Even better are forms of exercise such as brisk walking that allow you time to stop and smell the roses, another helpful activity to calm and focus your mind. Try finding a form of exercise that you enjoy. That way you are far more likely to keep it up and enjoy its detoxing benefits. And make it fun: I love listening to music when I go to the gym, which can turn an exercise routine into a really fun thing. Music lifts the spirit. It also activates massive integration in the brain, raising your gift to new heights.

While you are planning the fun and exercise into your life to unblock those toxic seriousness and toxic health choices, look at your daily and weekly life schedule to see if it's normal. If you are anything like me, you will need help with this. I tend to be a workaholic and will buzz from one activity to the next pushing from work into time with my children and research and writing and teaching and forgetting to rest and take some "me time." But I know it's important because if I don't take a break my gift will stop operating. It's good to work hard and go the extra mile, but balance is necessary. I have taken my own advice!

The ever-increasing pace of life is called the "acceleration syndrome," and it is causing a global epidemic of hurry sicknesses. One of the symptoms is the dizzying speed at which we live and the amount of living we are forcing into our lives.

Every organ and muscle in our bodies have a sympathetic (stressed) state and a parasympathetic (relaxed) state. Both of these systems are part of the autonomic nervous system. Researchers at the Institute of HeartMath (an organization that researches the effects of positive emotions on physiology, quality of life and performance) have found that the toxic emotions experienced as a result of this "busy-rush syndrome" cause disruptions to the autonomic nervous system that lead to erratic heart rhythms (among a myriad of other health problems).[19]

If you take the time to do things that generate healthy thoughts and their positive emotions, such as love, respect and kindness, the result will be more coherent heart rhythms. This rhythm is a balance between the sympathetic (accelerates the heartbeat) and the parasympathetic (slows down the heartbeat) nervous systems. Therefore, relaxing is not just a luxury, it's a necessity. You need to balance the sympathetic and parasympathetic systems. Toxic seeds will throw this balance off and predispose you to sickness.

Many "solutions" offered, such as time management and learning to delegate and prioritize, are having the opposite effect. They can actually increase the pace of life even more, creating a time squeeze in which we are encouraged to cram even more into an hour. Some of these solutions only aggravate the problem they are supposed to be addressing.

They make you time poor, and that poverty is extending to your thought life and your gift. Your time is precious, and it belongs only to you. Every day you make choices about how you are going to spend your time. Learning to spend it wisely is an important part of controlling your thoughts.

The next time you think you don't have time for fun or exercise or relaxation, think again. The reality is simply that you have chosen to fill your time with activities and things other than exercise and relaxation. If you constantly focus on the little things, you may ignore the big things that ultimately determine your health, success and happiness.

If you don't build relaxation into your lifestyle you will become a less effective thinker, defeating your ability to accomplish your gift. In fact, for the brain to function like it should, it needs regroup consolidation time. If it doesn't get this, it will send out signals in the form of high-level stress hormones some of which are adrenalin and cortisol. If these chemicals constantly flow they create a "white noise" effect that increases anxiety and blocks clear thinking and the processing of information. Your body will suffer as well.

That's why we must break the gift-blocker of toxic seriousness, health and schedules by:

1. Using the discomfort zones to help identify and acknowledge if you are too serious, not resting enough and in toxic health patterns.
2. Using the frontal lobe to stand outside of ourselves and evaluate how we can change this.
3. Rewiring.
4. Never doing this without prayer and the help of the Holy Spirit.

Use Part Three to help with these. Relaxation is never a waste of time when it comes to unblocking your gift.

CHAPTER TWENTY-FIVE:
{TOXIC UNFORGIVENESS AS A GIFT-BLOCKER}

After learning about the other eleven gift-blockers, it may seem a little overwhelming that there is such opportunity for toxic seeds to be planted in our lives. That's why this last gift-blocker is so important – uprooting toxic unforgiveness and transplanting forgiveness in its place.

When I become angry or frustrated or irritated or upset or worked up over anyone or anything, who is the one really affected? Me, I am the one most affected.

Toxic thoughts, with their attached toxic emotions, are toxic seeds of unforgiveness that have been planted in the soil of fear and are being constantly watered by the almost addictive attention we give them. God says "cast all your anxiety on Him" (1 Peter 5:7 NIV); ruminating continuously will not make them better but worse. God knew this, which is why He gave us that Scripture.

Remember what I said in earlier chapters: each time something is brought into consciousness it will change in some way by getting worse or better.

In addition, there is all the neurochemistry attached to the thought cluster, which throws our bodies into a chemical frenzy when we plant toxic seeds and grow them. When we don't forgive and when we hang onto pain and events, we are growing those toxic seeds.

So if someone told you that you were no good or you were misrepresented or someone said something about you that wasn't true or you were accused of something you did not do or something bad happened to you – all these will harm you mentally and physically if you hang onto them. They become toxic unforgiveness.

Sometimes it is so difficult to let go of those unbelievable and unjust things that happened to you. We feel that if we don't nurse them they won't get better. But that in itself is a lie from the enemy because they do get worse the more attention we pay to them!

The neuroplasticity of the brain will grow the toxic unforgiveness an even deeper root and the branches will get ever more pervasive – much the way a briar will choke out the plants in a garden if not controlled.

The worldly approach is to indulge, speak about, tear apart and wallow. But this does not bring healing; it brings destruction because of all the neurological and neurochemical reactions taking place in your body. We need to acknowledge and repent for hanging on, and then we need to forgive. Forgiveness is not excusing the behavior, but it is placing the situation into God's hands.

The more attention you pay to a thought cluster, the more it will expand because attention creates the environment and conditions in your brain, necessary for change. This is good if the focus is on a healthy thought, but not good if it is an unhealthy thought of toxic unforgiveness. The attention can be likened to the watering of a plant – attention causes the neurochemical "water" to create proteins that build the thought into a stronger and bigger branch, increasing the levels of your stress.

Forgiveness is imperative to walking fully in your gift. God provided a way for us through forgiveness and has offered us an easy way out by casting all our cares on Him.

You cannot control the event, but you can control your reaction to the event. Repentance (for hanging on) and forgiveness are the ideal reactions to stop toxic unforgiveness from growing. We need to make it a habit to wire repentance and forgiveness into our brains.

God wants to protect our brains and does not want us getting worked up about little things.

Repentance and forgiveness stop nervousness and worry, leading to harmful anxiety disorders and all the other potential manifestations.

Repentance and forgiveness are how we recognize that we are not walking this road alone – you and God are in this together.

Repentance and forgiveness put God back on the throne so He can do what He is supposed to do and you can do what you are supposed to do.

To break the gift-blocker of toxic unforgiveness we must:

1.   Use the discomfort zones to help identify and acknowledge the gift-blocking toxic unforgiveness.
2.   Repent for growing toxic unforgiveness.
3.   Forgive, yourself and others.
4.   Rewire
5.   Never do this without prayer and the help of the Holy Spirit – like any process, overcoming this gift blocker will change your life.

Summary

When the seeds of toxic thoughts, emotions, words, choices, dreams, unforgiveness, love, touch, health, seriousness and schedules are "planted and watered" in the soil of fear, they take root in a powerful way. Sometimes it is difficult to recognize that even a small seed can grow to become a significant gift-blocker.

However, as you have seen from the previous chapters, this is exactly what happens. All the gift blockers grow from a tiny seed planted somewhere, somehow, at sometime. They become watered by the attention we give them with our thoughts and, unless dealt with, grow into gift-blockers and produce bad fruit in our lives.

This is where Romans 7:15-26 is so helpful:

Romans 7:15-25 (The Message)

14-16 I can anticipate the response that is coming: "I know that all God's commands are spiritual, but I'm not. Isn't this also your experience?" Yes. I'm full of myself — after all, I've spent a long time in sin's prison. What I don't understand about myself is that I decide one way, but then I act another, doing things I absolutely despise. So if I can't be trusted to figure out what is best for myself and then do it, it becomes obvious that God's command is necessary.

17-20 But I need something more! For if I know the law but still can't keep it, and if the power of sin within me keeps sabotaging my best intentions, I obviously need help! I realize that I don't have what it takes. I can will it, but I can't do it. I decide to do good, but I don't really do it; I decide not to do bad, but then I do it anyway. My decisions, such as they are, don't result in actions. Something has gone wrong deep within me and gets the better of me every time.

21-23 It happens so regularly that it's predictable. The moment I decide to do good, sin is there to trip me up. I truly delight in God's commands, but it's pretty obvious that not all of me joins in that delight. Parts of me covertly rebel, and just when I least expect it, they take charge.

24I've tried everything and nothing helps. I'm at the end of my rope. Is there no one who can do anything for me? Isn't that the real question?

25The answer, thank God, is that Jesus Christ can and does. He acted to set things right in this life of contradictions where I want to serve God with all my heart and mind, but am pulled by the influence of sin to do something totally different.

When we rewire, we are planting new seeds and watering and growing new thoughts.

Like any process, it can take time, but with the neuroplasticity God has so graciously built into the function of our brain, you really can achieve lasting change. Never forget: you can change your brain and release your gift. So, plant new seed and walk in confidence that change can happen—we can see it in Scripture, just as we can in science.

CONCLUSION

What scientists and researchers, with their new tools and techniques of evaluation and analysis have discovered recently may leave you stunned. This book was birthed in that arena to stun you and excite you and motivate you into recognizing the truth: God has given you the gift of free will empowering you to be in control of the very thing that creates everything about who you are: your thought life.

He has truly given you a piece of eternity.

May you take this gift, your piece of eternity, and use it for the great things it was designed for and take your place in changing the world.

Now that you've discovered the structure of your gift and how to identify any potential gift-blockers that may be standing in your way of walking fully in your gift, what's next? Since your gift is unique, how you process the potential of your gift will also be unique.

If you would like to concentrate on overcoming any gift-blockers that you have identified, I would encourage you to read my book, *Who Switched Off My Brain? Controlling Toxic Thoughts and Emotions*, for more guidance and a step-by-step process.

And, because I think it is so important for you to have the tools for lasting change, I have developed a series of exercises to help you break free from toxic thinking and launch into your gift.

So, I invite you to visit the secure site www.drleaf.net/detox online and download this special guide as my gift to you.

Reader Bonus!

Online Detox Guide

After you have discovered the structure of your unique gift, don't let gift-blockers stand in the way of who you were created to be. I have developed a unique devotional to help you take the first steps toward walking fully in your gift.

Love,
Caroline

To access this powerful resource, simply enter this secure site in your web browser: **drleaf.net/detox**

An exclusive guide to breaking toxic patterns and stepping into your gifting is available online, free for download.

Launch into your future with confidence!

ACKNOWLEDGEMENTS

I want to thank the amazing team at Inprov for making this book happen, including all those whose names aren't included here.

I especially want to thank my friend and editor, Carolyn – you have really used your gift with excellence. You are amazing, and I am blessed to work with you.

Thanks to Amy Williams, Cody Phillips, Leyna Hutchinson, Jessica Arnold, and Renee Cook, for all the hours and effort you have put into getting this project together in record time and with such a spirit of excellence.

Thanks to Jimmy and Terry – you both use your gifts to bring out others' gifts. Thank you both for believing in me.

Thanks to Dr. Peter Amua-Quarshie who spent hours talking through the manuscript and getting excited along with me as we explored the magnificent workings of the brain. Thanks for sharing my passion and for your expertise.

Thanks to Kayla, my assistant, who spent many hours running around with all the behind-the-scenes things that happen when a book is written; thank you for listening to my ideas and reading the manuscript. You have really helped me.

Thanks to my husband, Mac, who spent hours listening to my ideas, helping me with the research and reading and rereading my manuscript. I am so grateful for the oneness we experienced in this project to reach out to others together with this message of hope.

And last, but not least, I want to thank my four amazing children who sacrificed so much "mom-time" so I could finish this book. Jessica, Dominique, Jeffrey and Alexy, you fill my heart with joy.

Also by Dr. Caroline Leaf

WHO SWITCHED OFF
MY
BRAIN?

controlling **toxic** thoughts and emotions

REVISED EDITION

Over 200,000 copies in print!

Plus bonus

dr. caroline leaf

Want to learn more about breaking the cycle of toxic thinking?

In her ground-breaking book, *Who Switched Off My Brain? Controlling Toxic Thoughts and Emotions*, Dr. Caroline Leaf illustrates a step-by-step method for sweeping away areas of toxic thinking.

Who Switched Off My Brain? is now available online and at retailers near you!

END NOTES

END NOTES:

Part One

1.

- Amua-Quarshie, P. 2009. <u>Basalo-Cortical Interactions: The role of the basal forebrain in attention and Alzheimer's disease</u>. Unpublished Master's thesis. Rutgers University. Newark, NJ. http://news.rutgers.edu/focus/issue.2008-03-26.6300207636/article.2008-03-26.8293146433.
- Allen, D. & Amua-Quarshie, P. et.al. 2004. <u>Mental Health at Work (White Paper)</u> by Pecan Ltd, Peckham. London, UK. http://www.pecan.org.uk/Group/Group.aspx?id=41212R.
- Bach-y-Rita, P. & Collins, C.C. et al 1969. "Vision Substitution by Tactile Image Projection in Nature." 221(5184): 963-64.
- Beauregard, M. & O'Leary, D. 2007. <u>The Spiritual Brain</u>. Harper Collins. NY.
- Brain and Mind Symposium. Columbia University. 2004. http://c250.columbia.edu/c250_events/symposia/brain_mind/brain_mind_vid_archive.html.
- Damasio, A. R. 1999. <u>The Feeling of What Happens: Body and motion in the making of consciousness</u>. Harcourt, Brace & Company. NY.
- Decety, J., & Grezes, J. 2006. "The Power of Simulation: Imagining one's own and other's behavior." <u>Brain Research</u>. 1079, 4-14.
- Dispenza, J. 2007. "Evolve Your Brain: The science of changing your brain." Health Communications, Inc. FL.
- Doidge, N. 2007. <u>The Brain that Changes Itself: Stories of personal triumph from the frontiers of brain science</u>. Penguin Books. USA.
- Diamond, M. & Hopson, J. 1999. "How to Nurture Your Child's Intelligence, Creativity and Healthy Emotions from Birth through Adolescence." <u>Magic Trees of the Mind</u>. Penguin. USA.
- Kandel, E.R. 2006. <u>In Search of Memory: The emergence of a new science of mind</u>. W.W. Norton & Company. NY.
- Gardner, H. 1985. <u>Frames of Mind</u>. Basic Books. NY.

2.

- Leaf, C.M. 1997. "The Mind Mapping Approach: A model and framework for Geodesic Learning." Unpublished D. Phil Dissertation, University of Pretoria. Pretoria, SA.
- Leaf, C.M. 2005. <u>Switch on Your Brain: Understand your unique intelligence profile and maximize your potential</u>. Tafelberg. Cape Town, SA.
- Leaf, C.M. 2008. <u>Switch on Your Brain 5 Step Learning Process</u>. Switch on Your Brain USA. Dallas, TX.
- Iran-Nejad, A. 1987. "The Schema: A long-term memory structure of a transient functional pattern." in Teireny, R.J., Anders, P. & Mitchell, J.N. (Eds.) <u>Understanding Reader is Understanding</u>. pp. 109-128. Lawrence Erlbaum & Associates. Hillsdale, NJ.
- Iran-Nejad, A. 1989. "Associative & Nonassociative Schema Theories of Learning." <u>Bulletin of the Psychonomic Society</u>. 27 pp. 1-4.

3.

- Restak, R. 2009. <u>Think Smart: A neuroscientist's prescription for improving your brain performance</u>. Riverhead Books. NY.
- Bloom, F.E. 2007. Ed. <u>The Best of the Brain from Scientific American: Mind, matter and tomorrow's brain</u>. Dana Press. NY.
- Horstman, J. 2009. <u>The Scientific American Day in the Life of Your Brain</u>. Jossey-Bass. San Francisco, CA.
- Stengel, R. 2009. Ed. <u>TIME Your Brain: A User's Guide</u>. TIME Books. Des Moines, IA.

4.

- Restak, <u>Think Smart</u>.
- Bloom, <u>The Best of the Brain from Scientific American</u>.
- Horstman, <u>The Scientific American Day in the Life of Your Brain</u>.
- Stengel, <u>TIME Your Brain</u>.

5.
- Restak, Think Smart.

6.
- Leaf, "The Mind Mapping Approach."
- Leaf, Switch on Your Brain: Understand your unique intelligence profile and maximize your potential.
- Leaf, Switch on Your Brain 5 Step Learning Process.
- Leaf, C.M., Uys, I.C. & Louw, B. 1998. "An Alternative Non-Traditional Approach to Learning: The Metacognitive-Mapping Approach." The South African Journal of Communication Disorders. 45, pp. 87-102

7.
- Diamond & Hopson, "How to Nurture Your Child's Intelligence, Creativity and Healthy Emotions from Birth through Adolescence."
- Dispenza, "Evolve Your Brain."

8.
- Diamond & Hopson, "How to Nurture Your Child's Intelligence, Creativity and Healthy Emotions from Birth through Adolescence."
- Dispenza, "Evolve Your Brain."

9.
- Doidge, The Brain that Changes Itself.
- Kandel, In Search of Memory.
- Leaf, C.M. 1990. "Mind Mapping: A therapeutic technique for closed head injury." Masters Dissertation, University of Pretoria. Pretoria, SA.

10.
- Leaf, "Mind Mapping."
- Leaf, "The Mind Mapping Approach."

11.
- Lipton, B. 2008. The Biology of Belief: Unleashing the power of consciousness, matter and miracles. Mountain of Love Productions. USA.

12.
- Diamond & Hopson, "How to Nurture Your Child's Intelligence, Creativity and Healthy Emotions from Birth through Adolescence."

13.
- Doidge, The Brain that Changes Itself.

14.
- Merzenich, "Cortical Plasticity Contributing to Childhood Development."
- Merzenich, http://merzenich.positscience.com/.
- Shephred, Bob. "The Plastic Brain: Part 2." UAB Online Magazine. 2009. http://www.uab.edu/uabmagazine/2009/may/plasticbrain2.

15.
- Merzenich, M.M. 2001. "Cortical Plasticity Contributing to Childhood Development." McClelland, J.L. & Siegler R.S. (Eds.) Mecheanisms of Cognitive Development: Behavioral and neural perspectives. Lawrence Eribaum Associates. Mahwah, NJ.
- Merzenich, M. 2009. http://merzenich.positscience.com/.

16.
- "Ghost in Your Genes." http://www.pbs.org/wgbh/nova/genes/.
- Restak, R. 2000. "Mysteries of the Mind." National Geographic Society.

17.
- Nader, K., Schafe, G.E. et al. 2000. "Fear Memories Require Protein Synthesis in the Amygdala for Reconsolidation after Retrieval." Nature. 406(6797): 722-26.

18.
- "Ghost in Your Genes." http://www.pbs.org/wgbh/nova/genes/.
- Restak, "Mysteries of the Mind."

19.
- Lipton, The Biology of Belief.
- Dispenza, "Evolve Your Brain."

- Epigenetics. 2004. http://www.sciencemag.org/feature/plus/sfg/resources/res_epigenetics.dtl.
- Epigenetics. 2006. http://discovermagazine.com/2006/nov/cover.
- Epigenetics. 2006. http://www.ehponline.org/members/2006/114-3/focus.html.

20.
- Leaf, "The Mind Mapping Approach."
- Leaf, C.M. 1997. "The Development of a Model for Geodesic Learning: The Geodesic Information Processing Model." The South African Journal of Communication Disorders Vol. 44. pp. 53-70.
- Restak, K. 1979. The Brain: The last frontier. Doubleday. NY.
- Restak, "Mysteries of the Mind."
- Restak, Think Smart.
- Luria, A.R. 1980. Higher Cortical Functions in Man, 2nd Ed. Basic Books. NY.

- Gardner, H. 1981. The Quest for Mind: Piaget, Levi-Strauss, and the Structuralist Movement. University of Chicago Press. Chicago, IL and London.
- Gardner, Frames of Mind.
- Gardner, H. & Wolfe, D.P. 1983. "Waves and Streams of Symbolization." Rogers, D. & Slabada, J.A. (Eds.) The Acquisition of Symbolic Skills. Plenum Press. London.
- Pascuale-Leone, A. & Hamilton, R. 2001. "The Metamodal Organization of the Brain." Casanova, C. & Ptito. (Eds.) Progress in Brain Research Volume 134. Elsevier Science. San Diego, CA.

21.
- Einstein, A. 1979. The Human Side: New glimpses from his archives. Princeton University Press. Princeton, NJ.
- Einstein, A. 1999. "Albert Einstein: Person of the century." TIME. Dec 31, 1999.

22.
- Lepore, F.E. 2001. "Dissecting Genius: Einstein's brain and the search for the neural basis of intellect." Cerebrum. http://www.dana.org/news/cerebrum/detail.aspx?id=3032.
- Edmonds, Molly. "How Albert Einstein's Brain Worked." http://health.howstuffworks.com/einsteins-brain1.htm.

23.
- Lepore, "Dissecting Genius."
- Edmonds, "How Albert Einstein's Brain Worked."

24.
- Lepore, "Dissecting Genius."
- Edmonds, "How Albert Einstein's Brain Worked."

25.
- Einstein, The Human Side.
- Einstein, "Albert Einstein."
- Edmonds, "How Albert Einstein's Brain Worked.
- Kruszelnicki, 2004. Karl S. "Einstein Failed School." http://www.abc.net.au/science/articles/2004/06/23/1115185.htm.

26.
- Edmonds, "How Albert Einstein's Brain Worked."

27.
- Edmonds, "How Albert Einstein's Brain Worked."

Part Two

1.
- Leaf, "The Mind Mapping Approach."
- Gardner, Frames of Mind.
- Gazzaniga, M.S. 2004. (Ed.) The New Cognitive Neurosciences. Bradford Books. The MIT Press
- Feldman, D. 1980. Beyond Universals in Cognitive Development. Ablex Publishers. Norwood, NJ.
- Saloman, G. 1979. Interaction of Media, Cognition and Learning. Jossey-Bass. San Francisco, CA.

2.
- Leaf, "The Mind Mapping Approach."
- Gardner, Frames of Mind.
- Gazzaniga, The New Cognitive Neurosciences.
- Feldman, Beyond Universals in Cognitive Development.
- Saloman, Interaction of Media, Cognition and Learning.

3.
- Leaf, "The Mind Mapping Approach."
- Gardner, Frames of Mind.
- Gazzaniga, The New Cognitive Neurosciences.
- Feldman, Beyond Universals in Cognitive Development.
- Saloman, Interaction of Media, Cognition and Learning.
- Fodor, J. 1983. The Modularity of Mind. MIT/Bradford. Cambridge.

4.
- Dispenza, "Evolve Your Brain."
- Lipton, The Biology of Belief.
- Kandel, E.R, Schwartz, J.H. & Jessell, T.M. (Eds.). 1995. Essentials of Neural Science and Behavior. Appleton & Lange. USA.
- Hamerhoff, Stuart. http://www.hameroff.com/publications.html.
- Merkle, R.C. 1989. "Energy Limits to the Computational Power of the Human Brain in Foresight Update (6)."
- Revolver Entertainment. 2005. "What the Bleep Do We Know?"

5.
- Leaf, "The Mind Mapping Approach."
- Leaf, "The Development of a Model for Geodesic Learning."

- Gardner, The Quest for Mind.
- Gardner, Frames of Mind.
- Gardner & Wolfe, "Waves and Streams of Symbolization."

6.
- Epigenetics. http://www.sciencemag.org/feature/plus/sfg/resources/res_epigenetics.dtl.
- Epigenetics. http://discovermagazine.com/2006/nov/cover.
- Epigenetics. http://www.ehponline.org/members/2006/114-3/focus.html.
- Szyf, Moshe. "Epigenetics." 2009. http://www.the-scientist.com/article/display/55843/.

7.
- Kandel, In Search of Memory.

8.
- Zaborszky, L. 2002. "The Modular Organization of Brain Systems. Basal forebrain; the Last frontier." Changing views of Cajal's neuron. Progress in Brain Research: (136) 359-372.
- Amua- Quarshie, P. 2009. Basalo-Cortical Interactions.

9.
- Dispenza, Evolve Your Brain.
- Lipton, The Biology of Belief.
- Hamerhoff, http://www.hameroff.com/publications.html.
- Merkle, "Energy Limits to the Computational Power of the Human Brain in Foresight Update (6)."
- Revolver Entertainment. "What the Bleep Do We Know?"

10.
- Diamond, S. & Beaumont, J. (Eds.) Hemisphere Function of the Human Brain. pp. 264-278.
- Diamond, M. 1988. Enriching Heredity: The impact of the environment on the brain. Free Press. NY.
- Diamond & Hopson, "How to Nurture Your Child's Intelligence, Creativity and Healthy Emotions from Birth through Adolescence."
- Diamond, M., Scheibel, A., Murphy, G. Jr. & Harvey, T. "On the Brain of a Scientist: Albert Einstein." Experimental Neurology. 1985;88(1):198-204.
- Rosenzweig, M.R. & Bennet, E.L. 1976. Neuronal Mechanisms of Learning and Memory. MIT Press. Cambridge, MA.
- Rosenzweig, E.S., Barnes, C.A., & McNaughton, B.L. 2002. "Making Room for New Memories." Nature Neuroscience. 5(1): 6-8.
- Doidge, The Brain that Changes Itself.
- Leaf, "Mind Mapping."
- Leaf, "The Mind Mapping Approach."
- Iran-Nejad, "The Schema."
- Iran-Nejad, "Associative & Nonassociative Schema Theories of Learning."
- Iran-Nejad, A. & Chissom, B. 1988. "Active and Dynamic Sources of Self-Regulation." Paper presented at the Annual Meeting of the American Psychological Association. Atlanta, GA.

11.
- Lepore, "Dissecting Genius."
- Galaburda, A. M. 1999. Albert Einstein's Brain. Lancet. 354: 182.
- Einstein, The Human Side.
- Einstein, "Albert Einstein."
- Edmonds, "How Albert Einstein's Brain Worked."
- Kruszelnicki, 2004. Karl S. "Einstein Failed School."

12.
- Gazzaniga, M.S. 1977. Handbook of Neuropsychology. Plenum. NY.
- Gazzaniga, The New Cognitive Neurosciences.
- Gardner, The Quest for Mind.
- Gardner, Frames of Mind.
- Gardner & Wolfe, "Waves and Streams of Symbolization."
- Leaf, "The Mind Mapping Approach."
- Saloman, Interaction of Media, Cognition and Learning.

Part 3

1.
- Pert, C. B. 1997. Molecules of Emotion: Why you feel the way you feel. Simon and Schuster. UK.
- Pert, C. et al. 1973. "Opiate Agonists and Antagonists Discriminated by Receptor Binding in the Brain." Science. (182): 1359.
- Dispenza, Evolve Your Brain.

2.
- Kandel, In Search of Memory.
- Kandel, E.R, Schwartz, J.H. & Jessell, T.M. (Eds.) 2000. Principles of Neural Science, 4th Ed. McGraw-Hill. NY.
- Kandel, Schwartz & Jessell, Essentials of Neural Science and Behavior.
- Kandel. 2000. http://nobelprize.org/nobel_prizes/medicine/laureates/2000/kandel-lecture.pdf.
- Kandel, E.R. 1998. "A New Intellectual Framework for Psychiatry." American Journal of Psychia-

try. 155(4): 457-69.
- Restak, The Brain.
- Restak, R. 2000. "Mysteries of the Mind." National Geographic Society.
- Restak, Think Smart.
- Horstman, The Scientific American Day in the Life of Your Brain.

3.
- Freeman, W.J. 1995. Societies of Brains: A study in the neuroscience of love and hate. Lawrence Erlbaum Associates. Hillsdale, NJ.
- Merzenich, http://merzenich.positscience.com/.
- Merzenich, "Cortical Plasticity Contributing to Childhood Development."

4.
- Freeman, Societies of Brains.
- Merzenich, http://merzenich.positscience.com/.
- Merzenich, "Cortical Plasticity Contributing to Childhood Development."

5.
- Dispenza, Evolve Your Brain.
- Horstman, The Scientific American Day in the Life of Your Brain.
- Kandel, In Search of Memory.
- Kandel, Schwartz & Jessell, Principles of Neural Science.
- Kandel, Schwartz & Jessell, Essentials of Neural Science and Behavior.
- Kandel, http://nobelprize.org/nobel_prizes/medicine/laureates/2000/kandel-lecture.pdf.
- Kandel, "A New Intellectual Framework for Psychiatry."
- Stengel, TIME Your Brain.
- Restak, The Brain.
- Restak, "Mysteries of the Mind."
- Restak, Think Smart.
- Bloom, The Best of the Brain from Scientific American.

6.
- Dispenza, Evolve Your Brain.
- Lipton, The Biology of Belief.
- Hamerhoff, http://www.hameroff.com/publications.html.
- Merkle, "Energy Limits to the Computational Power of the Human Brain in Foresight Update (6)."
- Revolver Entertainment. "What the Bleep Do We Know?"

7.
- Bloom, The Best of the Brain from Scientific American.
- Kandel, In Search of Memory.

8.
- Dispenza, Evolve Your Brain.

9.
- Bloom, The Best of the Brain from Scientific American.
- Kandel, In Search of Memory.

10.
- Bloom, The Best of the Brain from Scientific American.
- Kandel, In Search of Memory.

11.
- Dispenza, Evolve Your Brain.

12.
- Pert, Molecules of Emotion.
- Colbert, D. 2003. Deadly Emotions.

13.
- Dispenza, Evolve Your Brain.
- Pert, Molecules of Emotion.
- Colbert, Deadly Emotions.

14.
- Doidge, The Brain that Changes Itself.

15.
- Damasio, A. R. 1999. The Feeling of What Happens: Body and motion in the making of consciousness. Harcourt, Brace & Company. NY.
- Dispenza, Evolve Your Brain.
- Doidge, The Brain that Changes Itself.

16.
- Lipton, The Biology of Belief.
- Lipton, B.H., Bensch, K.G., et al. 1991. "Microvessel Endothelial Cell Transdifferentiation: Phenotypic Characterization." Differentiation 46: 117-133.
- Epigenetics. http://www.sciencemag.org/feature/plus/sfg/resources/res_epigenetics.dtl.
- Epigenetics. http://discovermagazine.com/2006/nov/cover.
- Epigenetics. http://www.ehponline.org/members/2006/114-3/focus.html.

- Kandel, In Search of Memory.
- Szyf, "Epigenetics."

17.
- Dispenza, Evolve Your Brain.
- Pert, Molecules of Emotion.

18.
- Colbert, Deadly Emotions.
- Lipton, The Biology of Belief.
- Lipton, Differentiation.
- Dispenza, Evolve Your Brain.

19.
- Amen, D.G. 2008. Magnificent Mind at Any Age. Harmony Books. USA.
- Amen, D.G. 1998. Change Your Brain Change Your Life. Three Rivers Press. NY.
- Damasio, The Feeling of What Happens.

20.
- Doidge, The Brain that Changes Itself.
- Kandel, In Search of Memory.

21.
- Epigenetics. http://www.sciencemag.org/feature/plus/sfg/resources/res_epigenetics.dtl.
- Epigenetics. http://discovermagazine.com/2006/nov/cover.
- Epigenetics. http://www.ehponline.org/members/2006/114-3/focus.html.
- Szyf, "Epigenetics."

22.
- Dispenza, Evolve Your Brain.
- Horstman, The Scientific American Day in the Life of Your Brain.

23.
- Dispenza, Evolve Your Brain.
- Horstman, The Scientific American Day in the Life of Your Brain.

24.
- Diamond, Scheibel, Murphy & Harvey, "On the Brain of a Scientist."
- Kandel, In Search of Memory.
- Kandel, Schwartz, & Jessell, Principles of Neural Science.
- Kandel, Schwartz, & Jessell, Essentials of Neural Science and Behavior.
- Kandel. http://nobelprize.org/nobel_prizes/medicine/laureates/2000/kandel-lecture.pdf.
- Martin, K. 2009. www.biolchem.ucla.edu/labs/martinlab/links.htm.
- Martin, K. 2009. http://www.foxnews.com/story/0,2933,529187,00.html.

25.
- Kandel, In Search of Memory.

26.
- Nader & Schafe, Nature.
- Leaf, "The Mind Mapping Approach."

27.
- Lipton, The Biology of Belief.
- Kandel, In Search of Memory.

28.
- Lipton, The Biology of Belief
- Epigenetics. http://www.sciencemag.org/feature/plus/sfg/resources/res_epigenetics.dtl.
- Epigenetics. http://discovermagazine.com/2006/nov/cover.
- Epigenetics. http://www.ehponline.org/members/2006/114-3/focus.html.
- Szyf, "Epigenetics."

29.
- Doidge, The Brain that Changes Itself.
- "Ghost in Your Genes." http://www.pbs.org/wgbh/nova/genes/.
- Harvard Health Publications. 2009. https://www.health.harvard.edu/newsweek/Prevalence-and-treatment-of-mental-illness-today.html.
- Kopp, M.S. & Rethelyi, J. 2004. "Where Psychology Meets Physiology: Chronic stress and premature mortality – the Central-Eastern European health paradox." Brain Research Bulletin. 62: 351-367.
- Lipton, The Biology of Belief.
- Lipton, Differentiation.
- National Institute of Mental Health. 2009. www.nimh.nih.gov/health/topics/statistics/index.shtml.

Part Four

1.
- Roizen, M.F. & Mehmet, C.O. 2008. <u>You: The owner's manual</u>. HarperCollins. NY.
- Bloom, <u>The Best of the Brain from Scientific American</u>.
- Colbert, <u>Deadly Emotions</u>.

2.
- Leaf, C.M. 2009. <u>Who Switched Off My Brain? Controlling Toxic Thoughts and Emotions</u>. Revised edition. Inprov. Dallas, TX.

3.
- Eisenburger, N. 2008. "Understanding the Moderators of Physical and Emotional Pain: A neural systems-based approach. " <u>Psychological Inquiry</u> (19) 189-195.

4.
- Doidge, <u>The Brain that Changes Itself</u>.

5.
- Freeman, <u>Societies of Brains: A study in the neuroscience of love and hate</u>.
- Merzenich, http://merzenich.positscience.com/.
- Merzenich, "Cortical Plasticity Contributing to Childhood Development."

6.
- Freeman, <u>Societies of Brains</u>.
- Merzenich, http://merzenich.positscience.com/.
- Merzenich, "Cortical Plasticity Contributing to Childhood Development."

7.
- Jouvet, M. 2009. "Working on a Dream." <u>Nature Neuroscience</u> (12) 811.
- Restak, "Mysteries of the Mind."
- Hobson, A. 2002. <u>Dreaming: An Introduction to the science of sleep</u>.

8.
- Jouvet, "Working on a Dream."
- Restak, "Mysteries of the Mind."
- Hobson, <u>Dreaming</u>.
- Solms, M. 1997. "The Neuropsychology of Dreams: A clinico-anatomical study." Lawrence Erlbaum.

9.
- Jouvet, "Working on a Dream."
- Restak, "Mysteries of the Mind."
- Hobson, <u>Dreaming</u>.
- Solms, "The Neuropsychology of Dreams."

10.
- Jouvet, "Working on a Dream."
- Restak, "Mysteries of the Mind."
- Hobson, <u>Dreaming</u>.
- Solms, "The Neuropsychology of Dreams."

11.
- Braun, A. 1999. "The New Neuropsychology of Sleep" Commentary. <u>Neuro-Psychoanalysis</u>. (1) 196-201.

12.
- Solms, M. 1999. http://www.abc.net.au/rn/talks/8.30/helthrpt/stories/s44369.htm.
- Solms, M. 2000. "Forebrain Mechanisms of Dreaming are Activated from a Variety of Sources." <u>Behavioral and Brain Sciences</u>. 23 (6): 1035-1040; 1083-1121.
- Solms, "The Neuropsychology of Dreams."

13.
- Solms, http://www.abc.net.au/rn/talks/8.30/helthrpt/stories/s44369.htm.
- Solms, "Forebrain Mechanisms of Dreaming are Activated from a Variety of Sources."
- Solms, "The Neuropsychology of Dreams."

14.
- Plotsky, P.M. & Meaney, M.J. 1993. "Early Postnatal Experience Alters Hypothalamic Corticotrophin-releasing Factor (CRF) mRNA, Median Eminence CRF Content and Stress-induced Release in Adult Rats." <u>Molecular Brain Research</u>. 18:195-200.

15.
- Rizzolotti, G. 2008. http://www.scholarpedia.org/article/Mirror_neurons.

16.
- Colbert, <u>Deadly Emotions</u>.
- Fountain, D. 2000. <u>God, Medicine, and Miracles</u>: The spiritual factors in healing. Random House.
- Cousins, N. 1981. <u>Anatomy of an Illness as Perceived by the Patient</u>. Bantam, NY.

17.

- Laughter. 2007. http://thehealingpoweroflaughter.blogspot.com/2007/07/how-marx-brothers-brought-norman.html.
- Laughter. http://heyugly.org/LaughterOneSheet2.php.
- Cousins, <u>Anatomy of an Illness as Perceived by the Patient</u>.

18.

- Vaynman S. & Gomez-Pinilla. 2005. "License to Run: Exercise impacts functional plasticity in the intact and injured central nervous system by using neurotrophins." <u>Neurorehabilitation and Neural Repair</u>. 19(4): 283-95.

19.

- Heart Science. http://www.heartmath.org/research/science-of-the-heart.html.

RECOMMENDED READING

RECOMMENDED READING

The concepts I teach in this book cover a very wide spectrum and years of reading, researching and working with clients, in private practice and schools and business corporations. If I had to provide all the citations to document the origin of each fact for complete scientific scholarship that I have used, there would be almost as many citations as words. So I have used a little flexibility to write this book in a more popular style, helping me to communicate my message as effectively as I can. There are only a few citations in the actual text that are more general, and the book list that follows is less of a bibliography (which would be too long) and more of a recommended reading list of some of the great books and scientific articles I have used in my research.

1. Adams, H.B. & Wallace, B. 1991. "A Model for Curriculum Development: TASC." Gifted Education International. 7, pp. 194-213.
2. Alavi, A., Hirsch, L.J. 1991. "Studies of Central Nervous System Disorders with Single Photon Emission Computed Tomography and Positron Emission Tomography: Evolution over the past 2 decades." Semin. Nucl. Med. 21 (1), Jan.: 51-58.
3. Alesandrini, K.L. 1982. "Imagery – Eliciting Strategies and Meaningful Learning." Journal of Educational Psychology. 62, pp. 526-530.
4. Allen, D. & Amua-Quarshie, P. et.al. 2004. Mental Health at Work (White Paper) by Pecan Ltd, Peckham. http://www.pecan.org.uk/Group/Group.aspx?id=41212R. London.
5. Allport, D.A. 1980. "Patterns and Actions: Cognitive mechanisms and content specific." in Claxton, G.L. (Ed.) Cognitive Psychology: New Directions. Routledge & Kegan Paul. London.
6. Amen, D.G. 2008. Magnificent Mind at Any Age. Harmony Books. USA.
7. Amen, D.G. 1998. Change Your Brain Change Your Life. Three Rivers Press. NY.
8. Amend, A.E. 1989. "Defining and Demystifying Baroque, Classic and Romantic Music." Journal of the Society. for Accelerative Learning and Teaching. 14 (2), pp. 91-112.
9. Amua-Quarshie, P. 2009. Basalo-Cortical Interactions: The role of the basal forebrain in attention and alzheimer's disease. Unpublished Master's thesis. Rutgers University. Newark, NJ.
10. Amua-Quarshi, P. 2008. http://news.rutgers.edu/focus/issue.2008-03-26.6300207636/ article.2008-03-26.8293146433.
11. Anderson, J.R. 1985. Cognitive Psychology and Its Complications, 2nd Ed. W.H. Freeman. NY.
12. Arnheim, R. 1979. "Visual Thinking in Education." in Sheikll, A. and Shaffer, J. (Eds.) The Potential of Fantasy and Imagination. pp. 215-225. Brandon House. NY.
13. Atkins, R.C. 1990. Dr. Atkins Health Revolution. Houghton Mifflin Company. Boston, MA.
14. Atkins, R.C. 2003. Dr. Atkins New Diet Revolution. Ebury Press. London.
15. Atkins, R.C. 2003. New Diet Cook Book. Ebury Press. London.
16. Bach-y-Rita, P. & Collins, C.C. et al 1969. "Vision Substitution by Tactile Image Projection in Nature." 221(5184): 963-64.
17. Bancroft, W.J. "Accelerated Learning Techniques for the Foreign Language Classroom." Per Linguam. 1 (2), pp. 20-24.
18. Barker, J.A. 1987. Discovering the Future: A question of paradigms. Charterhouse Productions, S.A. Breweries. SA.
19. Bartlett, F.C. 1932. Remembering: A study in experimental and social psychology. Cambridge University Press. Cambridge.
20. Baxter, R., Cohen, S.B. & Ylvisaker, M. 1985. "Comprehensive Cognitive Assessment." in Ylvisaker, M. Head Injury Rehabilitation: Children and adolescents. pp. 247-275. College-Hill Press. CA.
21. Beauregard, M. & O'Leary, D. 2007. The Spiritual Brain. Harper Collins. NY.
22. Bereiter, L. 1985. "Toward a Solution of the Learning Paradox." Review of Educational Research. 55, pp. 201-225.
23. Berninger, V., Chen, A. & Abbot, R. 1988. "A Test of the Multiple Connections Model of Reading Acquisition." International Journal of Neuroscience. 42, pp. 283-295.
24. Bishop, J.H. 1989. "Why the Apathy in American High Schools?" Educational Researcher. 18 (1), pp. 6-10.
25. Block, N. & Dworkin, G. 1976. The I.Q. Controversy. Pantheon. NY.

26. Bloom, B.S. 1984. "The Z Sigma Problem: The search for methods of group instruction as effective as one-to-one tutoring." Educational Researcher. 13 (6), pp. 4-16.
27. Bloom, F.E. 2007. Ed. The Best of the Brain from Scientific American: Mind, matter and tomorrow's brain. Dana Press. NY.
28. Bloom, F.E. Beal, M.F et al. eds. 2003. The Dana Guide to Brain Health. Dana Press. NY.
29. Bloom, L. & Lahey, M. 1978. Language Development and Language Disorders. Wiley & Sons. Canada.
30. Boller, K. & Rovee-Collier, C. 1992. "Contextual Coding and Recording of Infants' Memories." Journal of Experimental Child Psychology. 53 (1), pp. 1-23.
31. Borkowski, J.G., Schneider, W. & Pressley, M. 1989. "The Challenges of Teaching Good Information Processing to the Learning Disabled Student." International Journal of Disability, Development and Education. 3 (3), pp. 169-185.
32. Botha, L. 1985. "SALT in Practice: A report on progress." Journal of the Society for Accelerative Learning and Teaching. 10 (3), pp. 197-199.
33. Botkin, J.W., Elmandjra, M. & Malitza, M. 1979. No Limits to Learning: Bridging the human gap: A report to the Club of Rome. Pergammon Press. Oxford and NY.
34. Boyle, P. 2009. http://esciencenews.com/articles/2009/06/15/having.a.higher.purpose.life.reduces. risk.death.among.older.adults.
35. Brain and Mind Symposium. Columbia University. 2004. http://c250.columbia.edu/c250_events/ symposia/brain_mind/brain_mind_vid_archive.html.
36. Bransford, J.D. 1979. Human Cognition. Wadsworth. Belmont, CA.
37. Braten, I. 1991. "Vygotsky as Precursor to Metacognitive Theory, II: Vygotsky as metacognitivist." Scandinavian Journal of Educational Research. 35 (4), pp. 305-320.
38. Braun, A. 1999. The New Neuropsychology of Sleep Commentary. Neuro-Psychoanalysis (1) 196-201.
39. Briggs, M.H. 1993. "Team Talk: Communication skills for early intervention teams." Journal of Childhood Communication Disorders. 15 (1), pp. 33-40.
40. Broadbent, D.E. 1958. Perception and Communication. Pergammon Press. London.
41. Brown, A.L. 1978. "Knowing When, Where and How to Remember: A problem of meta-cognition." in Glaser, R. (Ed.) Advances in Instructional Psychology. Erlbourne. Hillsdale, NJ.
42. Bunker, V.J., McBurnett, W.M. & Fenimore, D.L. 1987. "Integrating Language Intervention throughout the School Community." Journal of Childhood Communication Disorders. 11 (1), pp. 185-192.
43. Buzan, T. 1991. Use Both Sides of Your Brain. Plume. NY.
44. Buzan, T. 2000. Head First. Thorsons. London.
45. Buzan, T. & Dixon, T. 1976. The Evolving Brain. Wheaten & Co, Ltd. Exetar.
46. Buzan, T. & Keene, R. 1996. The Age Heresy. Ebury Press. London.
47. Bynum, J. 2002. Matters of the Heart. Charisma House. USA.
48. Byron, R. 1986. Behavior in Organizations: Understanding and managing the human side of work, 2nd Ed. Allyn & Bacon. Boston, MA.
49. Byron, R. & Byrne, D. 1984. Social Psychology: Understanding human interaction, 4th Ed. Allyn & Bacon. Boston, MA.
50. Calvin, W. & Ojemann, G. 1994. Conversations with Neil's Brain. Addison-Wesley. Reading, MA.
51. Campbell, B., Campbell, L. and Dickinson, D. 1992. "Teaching and Learning through Multiple Intel-ligences." New Horizons for Learning. Seattle, WA.
52. Campione, J.C., Brown, A.L. & Bryant, N.R. 1985. "Individual Differences in Learning and Memory." in Sternberg, R.J. (Ed.) Human Abilities: An information processing approach. pp. 103-126. West Freeman. NY.
53. Capra, F. 1982. "The Turning Point: A new vision of reality." The Futurist. 16 (6), pp. 19-24.
54. Caskey, O. 1986. "Accelerating Concept Formation." Journal of the Society for Accelerative Learning andTeaching. 11 (3), pp. 137-145.
55. Chi, M. 1985. "Interactive Roles of Knowledge and Strategies in the Development of Organized Sorting and Recall." in Chipman, S.F., Segal, J.W. & Glaser, R. (Eds.) Thinking and Learning Skills Vol 2. Lawrence Erlbaum & Assoc. Hillsdale, NJ.
56. Childre, D. & Martin, H. 1999. The Heartmath Solution. Harper-Collins. San Francisco, CA.
57. Clancey, W. 1990. "Why Today's Computers Don't Learn the Way People Do." Paper presented at the Annual Meeting of the American Educational Research Association. Boston, MA.
58. Clark, A.J. 2005. "Forgiveness: A neurological model." Medical Hypotheses. (65):649-54.
59. Cloete, P. 2003. Lecture Series. Tel: (044) 884 0863.
60. Colbert, D. 2001. The Bible Cure for Memory Loss. Siloam Press. FL.
61. Colbert, D. 2003. Deadly Emotions: Understand the mind-body-spirit connection that can heal or destroy you. Thomas Nelson. Nashville, TN.
62. Concise Oxford Dictionary, 9th Ed. 1995. Oxford University Press. Oxford.
63. Cook, N.D. 1984. "Colossal Inhibition: The key to the brain code." Behavioral Science. 29, pp. 98-110.
64. Costa, A. L. 1984. "Mediating the Metacognitive." Educational Leadership. 42 (3), pp. 57-62.
65. Cousins, N. 1981. Anatomy of an Illness as Perceived by the Patient. Bantam, NY.
66. Cousins, N. 1979. "Anatomy of an Illness as Perceived by the Patient." New England Journal of Medicine. 295(1976) 1458-63.
67. Crick, F. The Astonishing Hypothesis: The scientific search for the soul. Charles Scribner & Sons. NY.
68. Crick, F.H.C. 1981. "Thinking about the Brain." Scientific American. 241 (3), p. 228.

69. Damasio, A. R. 1999. The Feeling of What Happens: Body and motion in the making of consciousness. Harcourt, Brace & Company. NY.

70. Damico, J.S. 1987. "Addressing Language Concerns in the Schools: The SLP as consultant." Journal of Childhood Communication Disorders. 11 (1), pp. 17-40.

71. Dartigues, J-F. 1994. "Use It or Lose It." Omni. Feb. 1994, p. 34.

72. De Andrade, L.M. 1986. "Intelligence's Secret: The limbic system and how to mobilize it through suggestopedy." Journal of the Society for Accelerative Learning and Teaching. 11 (2), pp. 103-113.

73. De Capdevielle, B. 1986. "An Overview of Project Intelligence." Per Linguam. 2 (2), pp. 31-38.

74. Decety, J. & Grezes, J. 1996. "Neural Mechanisms Subserving the Perception of Human Actions." in http://www.scribd.com/doc/16500831/Neural-Mechanisms-Sub-Serving-the-Perception-of-Human-Actions-Decety-Grezes-1999.

75. Decety, J., & Grezes, J. 2006. "The Power of Simulation: Imagining one's own and other's behavior." Brain Research. 1079, 4-14.

76. Decety, J., & Jackson, P.L. 2006. "A Social Neuroscience Perspective of Empathy." Current Directions in Psychological Science. 15, 54-58.

77. Derry, S.J. 1990. "Remediating Academic Difficulties through Strategy Training: The acquisition of useful knowledge." Remedial and Special Education. 11 (6), pp. 19-31.

78. Dhority, L. 1991. The ACT Approach: The artful use of suggestion for integrative learning. PLS Verlag GmbH, An derWeide. Bremen, West Germany.

79. Diamond, M. 1988. Enriching Heredity: The impact of the environment on the brain. Free Press. NY.

80. Diamond, M. & Hopson, J. 1999. "How to Nurture Your Child's Intelligence, Creativity and Healthy Emotions from Birth through Adolescence." Magic Trees of the Mind. Penguin. USA.

81. **Diamond, M., Scheibel, A., Murphy, G. Jr. & Harvey, T. "On the Brain of a Scientist: Albert Einstein." Experimental Neurology. 1985;88(1):198-204.**

82. Dienstbier, R. 1989. "Periodic Adrenalin Arousal Boosts Health Coping." Brain-Mind Bulletin. 14(9a).

83. Diamond, S. & Beaumont, J. (Eds.) Hemisphere Function of the Human Brain. pp. 264-278.

84. Dispenza, J. 2007. "Evolve Your Brain: The science of changing your brain." Health Communications, Inc. FL.

85. Dobson, J. 1997. How to Build Confidence in Your Child. Hodder & Stoughton. GB.

86. Doidge, N. 2007. The Brain that Changes Itself: Stories of personal triumph from the frontiers of brain science. Penguin Books. USA.

87. Duncan, J., Seitz, R. & Kolodny, J. et al. 2000. "A Neural Basis for General Intelligence." Science. 289:457-460.

88. Edelman, G.M. & Mountcastle, V.B. (Eds.). The Mindful Brain. MIT Press. Cambridge, MA.

89. Edelman, G.M. & Tononi, G. 2000. A Universe of Consciousness: How matter becomes imagination. Basic Books. NY.

90. Edmonds, M. "How Albert Einstein's Brain Worked." http://health.howstuffworks.com/einsteins-brain1.htm.

91. Edwards, B. 1979. Drawing on the Right Side of the Brain. J.P. Torcher. Los Angeles, CA.

92. Einstein, A. 1999. "Albert Einstein: Person of the century." TIME. Dec. 31, 1999.

93. Einstein, A. 1979. The Human Side: New glimpses from his archives. Princeton University Press. Princeton, NJ.

94. Eisenburger, N. 2008. "Understanding the Moderators of Physical and Emotional Pain: A neural systems-based approach." Psychological Inquiry (19) 189-195.

95. Enchanted Loom. 1986. BBC Productions.

96. Entwistle, N. 1988. "Motivational Factors in Students' Approaches in Learning." in Schmeck, R.R. (Ed.) Learning Strategies and Learning Styles. pp. 21-51. Plenum. NY.

97. Entwistle, N.J. & Ramsdon, P. 1983. Understanding Student Learning. Croom Helm. London.

98. Epigenetics. 2004. http://www.sciencemag.org/feature/plus/sfg/resources/res_epigenetics.dtl.

99. Epigenetics. 2006. http://discovermagazine.com/2006/nov/cover.

100. Epigenetics. 2006. http://www.ehponline.org/members/2006/114-3/focus.html.

101. Eriksen, C.W. & Botella, J. 1992. "Filtering Versus Parallel Processing in RSVP Tasks." Perception and Psychophysics. 51 (4), pp. 334-343.

102. Erskine, R. 1986. "A Suggestopedic Math Project Using Non Learning Disabled Students." Journal of the Society for Accelerative Learning and Teaching. 11 (4), pp. 225-247.

103. Farah, M.J., Peronnet, F. et al. 1990. "Brain Activity Underlying Visual Imagery: Event related potentials during mental image generation." Journal of Cognitive Neuroscience. 1:302-16.

104. Faure, C. 1972. Learning to Be: The world of education today and tomorrow. UNESCO. Paris.

105. Feldman, D. 1980. Beyond Universals in Cognitive Development. Ablex Publishers. Norwood, NJ.

106. Feuerstein, R. 1980. Instrumental Enrichment: An intervention program for cognitive modifiability. University Park Press. Baltimore, MD.

107. Feuerstein, R., Jensen, M., Roniel, S. & Shachor, N. 1986. "Learning Potential Assessment." Assessment of Exceptional Children. Haworth Press, Inc.

108. Flavell, J. H. 1978. "Metacognitive Development." in Scandura, J.M. & Brainerd, C.J. (Eds.) Structural/Process Theories of Complete Human Behaviour. Sijthoff & Noordoff. The Netherlands.

109. Flavell, P. 1963. The Developmental Psychology of Jean Piaget. Basic Books. NY.

110. Fodor, J. 1983. The Modularity of Mind. MIT/Bradford. Cambridge.

111. Forgiveness. 2004. https://www.health.harvard.edu/press_releases/power_of_forgiveness.

112. Forgiveness. 2005. http://www.aolhealth.com/conditions/five-for-2005-five-reasons-to-forgive.
113. Fountain, D. 2000. God, Medicine, and Miracles: The spiritual factors in healing. Random House.
114. Franzsen, S. 2003. Lecture series. Pretoria, SA.
115. Frassinelli, L., Superior, K. & Meyers, J. 1983. "A Consultation Model for Speech and Language Intervention." ASHA. 25 (4), pp. 25-30.
116. Freeman, W.J. 1995. Societies of Brains: A study in the neuroscience of love and hate. Lawrence Erlbaum Associates. Hillsdale, NJ.
117. Fuster, J.M. 2008. The Prefrontal Cortex, 4th Ed. Academic Press, London. http://www.elsevierdirect.com/product.jsp?isbn=9780123736444.
118. Galaburda, A. "Albert Einstein's Brain." Lancet. 1999; 354: 182.
119. Galton, F. 1907. Inquiries into Human Faculty and Its Development. L. M. Dent. London.
120. Gardner, H. 1985. Frames of Mind. Basic Books. NY.
121. Gardner, H. 1981. The Quest for Mind: Piaget, Levi-Strauss, and the Structuralist Movement. University of Chicago Press. Chicago, IL and London.
122. Gardner, H. & Wolfe, D.P. 1983. "Waves and Streams of Symbolization." in Rogers, D. & Slabada, J.A. (Eds.) The Acquisition of Symbolic Skills. Plenum Press. London.
123. Gazzaniga, M.S. 1977. Handbook of Neuropsychology. Plenum. NY.
124. Gazzaniga, M.S. 2004. (Ed.) The New Cognitive Neurosciences. Bradford Books. The MIT Press.
125. Gelb, M. 1988. Present Yourself. Jalmar Press. Los Angeles, CA.
126. Gerber, A. 1987. "Collaboration between SLP's and Educators: A continuity education process." Journal of Childhood Communication Disorders. 11(1-2): 107-125.
127. "Ghost in Your Genes." http://www.pbs.org/wgbh/nova/genes/.
128. Glaser, R. 1977. Adaptive Education: Individual diversity and learning. Holt, Rhinehort and Winston. NY.
129. Glasser, M.D. 1986. Control Theory in the Classroom. Harper & Row. NY.
130. Goldberg, E. & Costa, L.D. 1981. "Hemisphere Differences in the Acquisition and Use of Descriptive Systems." Brain and Language. 14, pp. 144-173.
131. Gould, S. 1973. "Commission on Nontraditional Study." Diversity by Design. Jossey-Bass. San Francisco, CA.
132. Gould, S. 1981. The Mismeasure of Man. W.W. Norton. NY.
133. Griffiths, D.E. 1964. "Behavioural Science and Educational Administration." 63rd Yearbook of the National Society for the Study of Education. NSSE. Chicago, IL.
134. Gungor, E. 2007. There is More to the Secret. Thomas Nelson. Nashville, TN.
135. Guyton, A.C & Halle, J.E. Textbook of Medical Physiology, 9th Ed. W.D. Saunders. Philadelphia, PA.
136. Haber, R.N. 1981. "The Power of Visual Perceiving." Journal of Mental Imagery. 5, pp. 1-40.
137. Halpern, S. & Savary, L. 1985. Sound Health: The music and sounds that make us whole. Harper & Row. San Francisco, CA.
138. Hamerhoff, Stuart. http://www.hameroff.com/publications.html.
139. Hand, J.D. 1986. "The Brain and Accelerative Learning." Per Linguam. 2 (2), pp. 2-14.
140. Hand, J.D. & Stein, B.L. 1986. "The Brain and Accelerative Learning, Part II: The brain and its functions." Journal of the Society for Accelerative Learning and Teaching. 11(3), pp. 149-163.
141. Harlow, H. 1998. http://www.pbs.org/wgbh/aso/databank/entries/bhharl.html.
142. Harrell, K.D. 1995. Attitude is Everything: A tune-up to enhance your life. Kendall/Hunt Publishing Company. USA.
143. Harrison, C.J. 1993. "Metacognition and Motivation." Reading Improvement. 28 (1), pp. 35-39.
144. Hart, L. 1983. Human Brain and Human Learning. Longman. NY.
145. Harvard. https://www.health.harvard.edu/topic/stress.
146. Harvard University Gazette. 1996. "Aging Brains Lose Less Than Thought." http://www.hno.harvard.edu/gazette/1996/10.03/AgingBrainsLose.html.
147. Harvard University Gazette. 2003. "Childhood Abuse Hurts the Brain." http://www.hno.harvard.edu/gazette/2003/05.22/01-brain.html.
148. Harvard University Gazette. 1998. "Sleep, Dreams and Learning." http://www.news.harvard.edu/gazette/1996/02.08/ResearchLinksSl.html.
149. Harvard Health Publications. 2009. "Positive Psychology: Harnessing the power of happiness, personal strength and mindfulness." https://www.health.harvard.edu/special_health_reports/Positive-Psychology.
150. Harvard Health Publications. 2009. https://www.health.harvard.edu/newsweek/Prevalence-and-treatment-of-mental-illness-today.htm.
151. Hatfied, R. 1994. http://faculty.plts.edu/gpence/PS2010/html/Touch%20and%20Human%20Sexuality.htm.
152. Hatfield, W. & Robert W. 1994. "Touch and Human Sexuality." in Bullough, V., Bullough, B. & Stein, A. (Eds.). Human Sexuality: An Encyclopedia. Garland Publishing. NY.
153. Hatton, G.I. 1997. "Function-related Plasticity in the Hypothalamus." Annual Review of Neuroscience. 20:375-97.
154. Hawkins, D.B. 2001. When Life Makes You Nervous: New and effective treatments for anxiety. Cook Communication. USA.
155. Hayman, J.L. 1975. "Systems Theory and Human Organization." in Zalatimo, Sulerman, D. & Sterman, P.J. (Eds.). A Systems Approach to Learning Environments. MEDED Projects, Inc. Roselle, NJ.

156. Heart Science. http://www.heartmath.org/research/science-of-the-heart.html.
157. Healy, J. "Why Kids Can't Think: Bottom Line." Personal. 13 (8), pp. 1-3.
158. Hinton, G.E. & Anderson, J.A. 1981. Parallel Models of Associate Memory. Erlsbaum. Hillsdale, NJ.
159. Hobson, A. 2002. Dreaming: An introduction to the science of sleep.
160. Hochberg, L.R., Serruya, G.M. et al. 2006. "Neuronal Ensemble Control of Prosthetic Devices by a Human with Tetraplegia." Nature. 442(7099): 164-71.
161. Holden, C. 1996. "Child Development: Small refugees suffer the effects of early neglect." Science. 305:1076-1077.
162. Holford, P. 1999. The 30-Day Fat Burner Diet. Piatkus. London.
163. Holford, P. 1997. The Optimum Nutrition Bible. Piatkus. London.
164. Holford, P. 2003. Optimum Nutrition for the Mind. Piatkus. London.
165. Holt, J. 1964. How Children Fail. Pitman. NY.
166. Horstman, J. 2009. The Scientific American Day in the Life of Your Brain. Jossey-Bass. San Francisco, CA.
167. Hubel, D.H. 1979. "The Brain." Scientific American. 24 (13), pp. 45-53.
168. Hunter, C. & Hunter F. 2008. Laugh Yourself Healthy. Christain Life. FL.
169. Hyden, H. 1977. "The Differentiation of Brain Cell Protein, Learning and Memory." Biosystems. 8(4), pp. 22-30.
170. Hyman, S.E. 2005. "Addiction: A disease of learning and memory." Am J Psychiatry. 162:1414-22.
171. Iaccino, J. 1993. Left Brain-Right Brain Differences: Inquiries, evidence and new approaches. Lawrence Erlbaum & Associates. Hillsdale, NJ.
172. Iran-Nejad, A. 1990. "Active and Dynamic Self-Regulation of Learning Processes." Review of Educational Research. 60 (4), pp. 573-602.
173. Iran-Nejad, A. 1989. "Associative & Nonassociative Schema Theories of Learning." Bulletin of the Psychonomic Society. 27 pp. 1-4.
174. Iran-Nejad, A. 1987. "The Schema: A long-term memory structure of a transient functional pattern." in Teireny, R.J., Anders, P. & Mitchell, J.N. (Eds.) Understanding Reader is Understanding. pp. 109-128. Lawrence Erlbaum & Associates. Hillsdale, NJ.
175. Iran-Nejad, A. & Chissom, B. 1988. "Active and Dynamic Sources of Self-Regulation." Paper presented at the Annual Meeting of the American Psychological Association. Atlanta, GA.
176. Iran-Nejad, A. & Ortony, A. 1984. "A Biofunctional Model of Distributed Mental Content, Mental Structures, Awareness and Attention." The Journal of Mind and Behaviour. 5, pp. 171-210.
177. Iran-Nejad, A., Ortony, A. & Rittenhouse, R.k. 1989. "The Comprehension of Metaphonical Uses of English by Deaf Children." American Speech-Language Association. 24, pp. 551-556.
178. Jacobs, B., Schall, M. & Scheibel, A.B. 1993. "A Quantitative Dendritic Analysis of Wernickes Area in Humans: Gender, hemispheric and environmental factors." Journal of Comparative Neurology. 327(1): 97-111.
179. Jacobs, B.L., Van Praag, H. et al. 2000. "Depression and the Birth and Death of Brain Cells." American Scientist. 88 (4):340-46.
180. Jensen, A. 1980. Bias in Mental Testing. Free Press. NY.
181. Jensen, E. 1995. Brain-Based Learning and Teaching. Process Graphix. South Africa.
182. Johnson, D.W., Johnson, R.T. & Holubec, E. 1986. Circles of Learning: Co-operation in the classroom. Interaction Book Company. Edina, MN.
183. Johnson, J.M. 1987. "A Case History of Professional Evolution from SLP to Communication Instructor." Journal of Childhood Communication Disorders. 11 (4), pp. 225-234.
184. Jorgensen, C.C. & Kintsch, W. 1973. "The Role of Imagery in the Evaluation of Sentences." Cognitive Psychology. 4, pp. 110-116.
185. Jouvet, M. 2009. "Working on a Dream." Nature Neuroscience (12) 811.
186. Kagan, A. & Saling, M. 1988. An Introduction to Luria's Aphasiology Theory and Application. Witwatersrand University Press. Johannesburg, SA.
187. Kalivas, P.W. & Volkow N.D. 2005. "The Neural Basis of Addiction: A pathology of motivation and choice." Am J Psychiatry. 162: 1403-1413.
188. Kandel, E.R. 1998. "A New Intellectual Framework for Psychiatry." American Journal of Psychiatry. 155(4): 457-69.
189. Kandel, E.R. 2006. In Search of Memory: The emergence of a new science of mind. W.W. Norton & Company. NY.
190. Kandel, E.R, Schwartz, J.H. & Jessell, T.M. (Eds.) 1995. Essentials of Neural Science and Behavior Appleton & Lange. USA.
191. Kandel, E.R, Schwartz, J.H. & Jessell, T.M. (Eds.) 2000. Principles of Neural Science, 4th Ed. McGraw-Hill. NY.
192. Kandel. 2000. http://nobelprize.org/nobel_prizes/medicine/laureates/2000/kandel-lecture.pdf.
193. Kaniels, S. & Feuerstein, R. 1989. "Special Needs of Children with Learning Difficulties." Oxford Review of Education. 15 (2), pp. 165-179.
194. Kaplan-Solms K. & Solms, M. 2002. Clinical Studies in Neuro-Psychoanalysis. Karnac. NY.
195. Kazdin, A.E. 1975. "Covert Modelling, Imagery Assessment and Assertive Behaviour." Journal of Consulting and Clinical Psychology. 43, pp.716-724.
196. Kimara, D. 1973. "The Assymmetry of the Human Brain." Scientific American. 228 (3), pp. 70-80.
197. Kimara, D. September 1992. "Sex Differences in the Brain." Scientific American. pp. 119-125.

198. King, D.F. & Goodman, K.S. 1990. "Whole Language Learning, Cherishing Learners and their Language." Language, Speech and Hearing Sciences in Schools. 21, pp. 221-229.
199. Kintsch, W. 1980. "Learning from Text, Levels of Comprehension, or Why Anyone Would Read a Story Anyway?" Poetics. 9, pp. 87-98.
200. Kline, P. 1990. Everyday Genius. Great Ocean Publishers. Arlington, VA.
201. Knowles, M. 1990. The Adult Learner: A neglected species. Gulf Publishing Company. Houston.
202. Kopp, M.S. & Rethelyi, J. 2004. "Where Psychology Meets Physiology: Chronic stress and premature mortality – the Central-Eastern European health paradox." Brain Research Bulletin. 62: 351-367.
203. Kosslyn, S.M. & Koenig, O. 1995. Wet Mind: The new cognitive neuroscience. Free. NY.
204. Kruszelnicki, 2004. Karl S. "Einstein Failed School." http://www.abc.net.au/science/ articles/2004/06/23/1115185.htm.
205. Kubzansky, L.D., Kawachi, A. et al. 1997. "Is Worrying Bad for Your Heart? A prospective study of worry and coronary heart disease in the normative aging study." Circulation. (94):818-24.
206. Lahaye, T. & Noebel, D. 2000. "Mind Siege." The Battle for Truth in the New Millennium. Word Publishing. TN.
207. Larsson, G. & Starrin, B. 1988. "Effect of Relaxation Training on Verbal Ability, Sequential Thinking and Spatial Ability." Journal of the Society of Accelerative Learning and Teaching. 13 (2), pp. 147-159.
208. Laughter. 2007. http://thehealingpoweroflaughter.blogspot.com/2007/07/how-marx-brothers-brought-norman.html.
209. Laughter. 2006. http://heyugly.org/LaughterOneSheet2.php.
210. Lazar, C. 1994. "A Review and Appraisal of Current Information on Speech/Language Alternative Service Delivery Models in Schools." Communiphon. 308, pp. 8-11.
211. Lazar, S.W. & Kerr, C.E. 2005. "Meditation Experience is Associated with Increased Cortical Thickness." NeuroReport. 16(17): 189-97.
212. Lea, L. 1980. Wisdom: Don't live life without it. Highland Books. Guilford, Surrey.
213. Leaf, C.M. 1985. "Mind Mapping as a Therapeutic Intervention Technique." Unpublished workshop manual.
214. Leaf, C.M. 1989. "Mind Mapping as a Therapeutic Technique." Communiphon. 296, pp. 11-15. South African Speech-Language-Hearing Association.
215. Leaf, C.M. 1990. "Teaching Children to Make the Most of Their Minds: Mind Mapping." Journal for Technical and Vocational Education in South Africa. 121, pp. 11-13.
216. Leaf, C.M. 1990. "Mind Mapping: A therapeutic technique for closed head injury." Masters Dissertation, University of Pretoria. Pretoria, SA.
217. Leaf, C.M. 1992. "Evaluation and Remediation of High School Children's Problems Using the Mind Mapping Therapeutic Approach." Remedial Teaching. Unisa, 7/8, September 1992.
218. Leaf, C.M., Uys, I.C. & Louw, B. 1992. "The Mind Mapping Approach (MMA): A culture and language-free technique." The South African Journal of Communication Disorders Vol. 40. pp. 35-43.
219. Leaf, C.M. 1993. "The Mind Mapping Approach (MMA): Open the door to your brain power: Learn how to learn." Transvaal Association of Educators Journal (TAT).
220. Leaf, C.M. 1997. "The Mind Mapping Approach: A model and framework for Geodesic Learning." Unpublished D. Phil Dissertation, University of Pretoria. Pretoria, SA.
221. Leaf, C.M. 1997. "The Development of a Model for Geodesic Learning: The Geodesic Information Processing Model." The South African Journal of Communication Disorders Vol. 44. pp. 53-70.
222. Leaf, C.M. 1997. "The Move from Institution Based Rehabilitation (IBR) to Community Based Rehabilitation (CBR): A paradigm shift." Therapy Africa. 1 (1) August 1997, p. 4.
223. Leaf, C.M. 1997. "An Altered Perception of Learning: Geodesic Learning." Therapy Africa. 1 (2), October 1997, p. 7.
224. Leaf, C.M., Uys, I. & Louw. B., 1997. "The Development of a Model for Geodesic Learning: The Geodesic Information Processing Model." The South African Journal of Communication Disorders. 44.
225. Leaf, C.M. 1998. "An Altered Perception of Learning: Geodesic Learning: Part 2." Therapy Africa. 2 (1), January/February 1998, p. 4.
226. Leaf, C.M., Uys, I.C. & Louw, B. 1998. "An Alternative Non-Traditional Approach to Learning: The Metacognitive-Mapping Approach." The South African Journal of Communication Disorders. 45, pp. 87-102.
227. Leaf. C.M. 2002. Switch on Your Brain with the Metacognitive-Mapping Approach. Truth Publishing.
228. Leaf, C.M. 2005. Switch on Your Brain: Understand your unique intelligence profile and maximize your potential. Tafelberg. Cape Town, SA.
229. Leaf, C.M. 2008. Switch on Your Brain 5 Step Learning Process. Switch on Your Brain USA. Dallas, TX.
230. Leaf, C.M. 2007. Who Switched Off My Brain? Controlling Toxic Thoughts and Emotions. Switch on Your Brain USA. Dallas, TX.
231. Leaf, C.M. 2009. Who Switched Off My Brain? Controlling Toxic Thoughts and Emotions. Revised edition. Inprov. Dallas, TX.
232. Leaf, C.M. 2007. "Who Switched Off My Brain? Controlling toxic thoughts and emotions." DVD series. Switch on Your Brain. Johannesburg, SA.

233. Leaf, C.M., Copeland M. & Maccaro, J. 2007. "Your Body His Temple: God's plan for achieving emotional wholeness." DVD series. Life Outreach International. Dallas, TX.
234. LeDoux, J. 2002. Synaptic Self: How our brains become who we are. NY.
235. Leedy, P.D. 1989. Practical Research: Planning and design. Macmillan. NY.
236. Lehmann, E.L. 1975. Non-Parametric: Statistical methods based on ranks. Holden-Day. CA.
237. Lepore, F.E. 2001. "Dissecting Genius: Einstein's brain and the search for the neural basis of intellect." Cerebrum. http://www.dana.org/news/cerebrum/detail.aspx?id=3032.
238. Leuchter, A.F., Cook, I.A. et al. 2002. "Changes in Brain Function of Depressed Subject During Treatment with Placebo." American Journal of Psychiatry. 159(1): 122-129.
239. Levy, J. 1985. "Interview." Omni. 7 (4).
240. Levy, J. 1983. "Research Synthesis on Right and Left Hemispheres: We think with both sides of the brain." Educational Leadership. 40 (4), pp. 66-71.
241. Lewis, R. 1994. "Report Back on the Workshop: Speech/language/hearing therapy in transition." Communiphon. 308, pp. 6-7.
242. Lipton, B. 2008. The Biology of Belief: Unleashing the power of consciousness, matter and miracles. Mountain of Love Productions. USA.
243. Lipton, B.H., Bensch, K.G., et al. 1991. "Microvessel Endothelial Cell Transdifferentiation: Phenotypic Characterization." Differentiation 46: 117-133.
244. "Love and Neuroscience." 2009. http://www.nature.com/nature/journal/v457/n7226/full/457148a.html.
245. Lozanov, G. 1978. Suggestology and Outlines of Suggestopedy. Gordon and Breach Science Publishers. NY.
246. Lozanov, G. & Gateva, G. 1989. The Foreign Language Educator's Suggestopaedic Manual. Gordon and Breach Science Publishers. Switzerland.
247. L.T.F.A. 1995. Unpublished Lecture Series on "Brain-Based Learning." Lead the Field Africa. SA.
248. Luria, A.R. 1980. Higher Cortical Functions in Man, 2nd Ed. Basic Books. NY.
249. Lutz, K.A. & Rigney, J.W. 1977. The Memory Book. Skin & Day. NY.
250. MacLean, P. 1978. "A Mind of Three Minds: Educating the triuine brain." 77th Yearbook of the National Society for the Study of Education. pp. 308-342. University of Chicago Press. Chicago, IL.
251. Margulies, N. 1991. Mapping Inner-Space. Zephyr Press. Tulson.
252. Martin, K. 2009. www.biolchem.ucla.edu/labs/martinlab/links.htm.
253. Martin, K. 2009. http://www.foxnews.com/story/0,2933,529187,00.html.
254. Marvin, C.A. 1987. "Consultation Services: Changing roles for the SLP's." Journal of Childhood Communication Disorders. 11 (1), pp. 1-15.
255. Maslow, A.H. 1970. Motivation and Personality. Harper & Row. NY.
256. Mastropieri, M.A. & Bakken, J.P. 1990. "Applications of Metacognition." Remedial and Special Education. 11 (6) 32-35.
257. Matheny, K.B. & McCarthy, J. 2000. Prescription for Stress. Harbinger Publications. USA.
258. McEwan, B.S. 1999. "Stress and Hippocampal Plasticity." Annual Review of Neuroscience. 22:105-22.
259. McEwan, B.S. & Lasley, E.N. 2002. The End of Stress as We Know It. National Academies Press. WA.
260. McEwan, B.S. & Seeman, T. 1999. "Protective & Damaging Effects of Mediators of Stress: Elaborating and testing the concepts of allostasis and allostatic load." Annals of the New York Academy of Sciences. 896:30-47.
261. McGaugh, J.L. & Intrioni-Collision, I.B. 1990. "Involvement of the Amygdaloidal Complex in Neuromodulatory Influences on Memory Storage." Neuroscience and Behavioral Reviews. 14 (4), pp. 425-431.
262. Merkle, R.C. 1989. "Energy Limits to the Computational Power of the Human Brain in Foresight Update (6)."
263. Merzenich, M. 2009. http://merzenich.positscience.com/.
264. Merzenich, M.M. 2001. "Cortical Plasticity Contributing to Childhood Development." in McClelland, J.L. & Siegler R.S. (Eds.) Mecheanisms of Cognitive Development: Behavioral and neural perspectives. Lawrence Eribaum Associates. Mahwah, NJ.
265. Meyer, J. 1995. The Battlefield of the Mind. Faith Words. USA.
266. Meyer, J. 2000. Life without Strife: How God can heal and restore troubled relationships. Charisma House. FL.
267. Miller, G.A. 1956. "The Magical Number Seven, Plus or Minus Two: Some limits on our capacity for processing information." Psychological Review, 63, pp. 81-97.
268. Miller, T. & Sabatino, D. 1978. "An Evaluation of the Educator Consultant Model as an Approach to Main Streaming." Exceptional Children, 45.
269. "Mind/Body Connection: How emotions affect your health." 2009. http://family doctor.org/online/famdocen/home/healthy/mental/782.html.
270. Mogilner, A., Grossman, J.A. et al. 1993. Somatosensory Cortical Plasticity in Adult Humans Revealed by Magneto Encephalography. Proceedings of the National Academy of Sciences, USA 90(8): 3593-97.
271. Montessori, M. 1989. The Absorbent Mind. Clio Press. Amsterdam.
272. Mountcastle, V. 1978. "An Organizing Principle for Cerebral Function: The unit module and the

distributed system." in McAllister. 2000. "Cellular and Molecular Mechanisms of Dendritic Growth." <u>Cerebral Cortex</u>, 10(10): 963-73. Oxford University Press.

273. Nader, K., Schafe, G.E. et al. 2000. "Fear Memories Require Protein Synthesis in the Amygdala for Reconsolidation after Retrieval." <u>Nature</u>. 406(6797): 722-26.

274. National Institute of Mental Health. 2009. www.nimh.nih.gov/health/topics/statistics/index.shtml.

275. Nelson, A. 1988. "Imagery's Physiological Base: The limbic system. A review paper." <u>Journal of the Society for Accelerative Learning and Teaching</u>. 13 (4), pp 363-371.

276. Nelson, R. (Ed.) 1992. <u>Metacognition Core Readings</u>. Allyn & Bacon. Needham Heights, MA.

277. Neuroplasticity Research. http://www.uab.edu/uabmagazine/2009/may/plasticbrain2.

278. Neuroscience Review. http://cumc.columbia.edu/dept/cme/neuroscience/neuro/speakers.html.

279. Newberg, A., D'Aquili, E. et al. 2001. "Why God Won't Go Away: Brain science and the biology of belief." Ballantine. NY.

280. Novak, J.D. & Gowin, B. 1984. <u>Learning How to Learn</u>. Cambridge University Press. Cambridge.

281. Nummela, R.M. & Rosengren, T.M. 1985. "Orchestration of Internal Processing." <u>Journal for the Society of Accelerated Learning and Teaching</u>. 10 (2), pp. 89-97.

282. Odendaal, M.S. 1985. "Needs Analysis of Higher Primary Educators in KwaZulu." <u>Per Linguam</u>, Special Issue No. 1. pp. 5-99.

283. Okebukola, P.A. 1992. "Attitudes of Educators Towards Concept Mapping and Vee-diagramming as Metalearning Tools in Science and Mathematics." <u>Educational Research</u>, 34 (3), pp. 201-212.

284. O'keefe, J. & Nadel, L. 1978. <u>The Hippocampus as a Cognitive Map</u>. Oxford University Press. NY.

285. Olivier, C. 1999. <u>Let's Educate, Train and Learn Outcomes-Based</u>. Benedic. Pretoria, SA.

286. Olsen, K.E. 1997. <u>Outcomes Based Education: An experiment in social engineering</u>. Christians for Truth. SA.

287. Ornstein, R.E. 1975. <u>The Psychology of Consciousness</u>. Penguin Books. NY.

288. Ornstein, R. 1997. <u>The Right Mind</u>. Harcourt, Brace and Company. Orlando, FL.

289. Palincsar, A.S. & Brown, A.L. 1984. "Reciprocal Teaching of Comprehension Fostering and Monitoring Activities." <u>Cognition and Instruction</u>. 1, pp. 117-175.

290. Palmer, L.L., Alexander, M. & Ellis, N. 1989. "Elementary School Achievement Results Following In-Service Training of an Entire School Staff in Accelerative Learning and Teaching: An interim report." <u>Journal of the Society for Accelerative Learning and Teaching</u>. 14 (1), pp. 55-79.

291. Paris, S.G. & Winograd, P. 1990. "Promoting Metacognition and Motivation of Exceptional Children." <u>Remedial and Special Education</u>. 11 (6), pp. 7-15.

292. Pascuale-Leone, A. & Hamilton, R. 2001. "The Metamodal Organization of the Brain." in Casanova, C. & Ptito. (Eds.) <u>Progress in Brain Research</u> Volume 134. Elsevier Science. San Diego, CA.

293. Paterniti, M. 2000. "Driving Mr. Albert: A trip across America with Einstein's Brain." The Dial Press. New York.

294. Paul-Brown, D. 1992. "Professional Practices Perspective on Alternative Service Delivery Models." <u>ASHA Bulletin</u>. 12.

295. Perlemutter, D. & Coleman, C. 2004. <u>The Better Brain Book</u>. Penguin Group. USA.

296. Pert, C. B. 1997. <u>Molecules of Emotion: Why you feel the way you feel</u>. Simon and Schuster. UK.

297. Pert, C. et al. 1973. "Opiate Agonists and Antagonists Discriminated by Receptor Binding in the Brain." <u>Science</u>. (182): 1359-61.

298. Peters, T. 2003. <u>Playing God? Genetic Determinism and Human Freedom</u>, 2nd Ed. Routledge. NY.

299. "The Pleasure Centers Affected by Drugs." http://thebrain.mcgill.ca/flash/i/i_03/i_03_cr/i_03_cr_par/i_03_cr_par.html.

300. Plotsky, P.M. & Meaney, M.J. 1993. "Early Postnatal Experience Alters Hypothalamic Corticotrophin-releasing Factor (CRF) mRNA, Median Eminence CRF Content and Stress-induced Release in Adult Rats." <u>Molecular Brain Research</u>. 18:195-200.

301. Policy Document, 2002. "Revised National Curriculum Statement Grades R-9." Department of Education. Pretoria, SA.

302. Praag, A.F., Schinder, B.R. et al. 2002. "Functional Neurogenesis in the Adult Hippocampus." <u>Nature</u>. 415(6875): 1030-34.

303. Pribram, K.H. 1971. <u>Languages of the Brain</u>. Brooks/Cole. Monterey, CA.

304. Pulvermuller, F. 2002. <u>The Neuroscience of Language</u>. Cambridge University Press.

305. Rajechi, D.W. 1982. <u>Attitudes: Themes and Advances</u>. Sinauer Associates. Sunderland, MA.

306. Ramachandran, V.S. & Blakeslee, S. 1998. <u>Phantoms in the Brain</u>. William Morrow. NY.

307. Redding, R.E. 1990. "Metacognitive Instruction: Trainers teaching thinking skills." <u>Performance Improvement Quarterly</u>. 3 (1), pp. 27-41.

308. Relax. 2005. http://www.scientificamerican.com/article.cfm?id=want-clear-thinking-relax&page=2.

309. Relaxation. 2005. http://www.scientificamerican.com/article.cfm?id=want-clear-thinking-relax.

310. Religion and Science. 2008. http://www.liebertonline.com/doi/abs/10.1089/acm.2007.0675.

311. Religion and Science. 2009. http://www.time.com/time/health/article\0,8599,1879016,00.html.

312. Restak, K. 1979. <u>The Brain: The last frontier</u>. Doubleday. NY.

313. Restak, R. 2000. "Mysteries of the Mind." <u>National Geographic Society</u>.

314. Restak, R. 2009. <u>Think Smart: A neuroscientists prescription for improving your brain performance</u>. Riverhead Books. NY.

315. Revolver Entertainment. 2005. "What the Bleep Do We Know?"
316. Rizzolotti, G. 2008. http://www.scholarpedia.org/article/Mirror_neurons.
317. Rogers, C.R. 1969. Freedom to Learn. Merrill. Columbus, OH.
318. Roizen, M.F. & Mehmet, C. O. 2008. You: The owner's manual. Harper-Collins. NY.
319. Rosenfield, I. 1988. The Invention of Memory. Basic Books. NY.
320. Rosenzweig, M.R. & Bennet, E.L. 1976. Neuronal Mechanisms of Learning and Memory. MIT Press. Cambridge, MA.
321. Rosenzweig, E.S., Barnes, C.A., & McNaughton, B.L. 2002. "Making Room for New Memories." Nature Neuroscience. 5(1): 6-8.
322. Rozin, P. 1975. "The Evolution of Intelligence and Access to the Cognitive Unconscious." Progress in Psychobiology and Physiological Psychology. 6, pp. 245-280.
323. Russell, P. 1986. The Brain Book. Routledge & Kegan Paul. London.
324. Rutherford, R. & Neethling, K. 2001. Am I Clever or Am I Stupid? Carpe Diem Books. Van-derbijlpark.
325. Sagan, C. 1977. The Dragons of Eden. Random House. NY.
326. Saloman, G. 1979. Interaction of Media, Cognition and Learning. Jossey-Bass. San Francisco, CA.
327. Samples, R.E. 1975. "Learning with the Whole Brain." Human Behavior. 4, pp. 16-23.
328. Sapolsky, R.M. 1996. "Why Stress is Bad for Your Brain." Science. 273(5276): 749-50.
329. Sarno, J. 1999. The Mind-Body Prescription. Werner Books. NY.
330. Sarter, M., Hasselmo, M.E., Bruno, J.P. and Givens, B. 2005. "Unraveling the Attentional Functions of Cortical Cholinergic Inputs: Interactions between signal-driven and cognitive modulation of signal detection." Brain Res Brain Res Rev., 48(1): 98-111.
331. Schallert, D.L. 1982. "The Significance of Knowledge: A synthesis of research related to schema theory." in Otto, W. & White, S. (Eds.) Reading Expository Material. pp. 13-48. Academic. NY.
332. Schneider, W. & Shiffrin, R.M. 1977. "Controlled and Automatic Information Processing: I: Detection, search and attention." Psychological Review. 88, pp. 1-66.
333. Schon, D.A. 1971. Beyond the Stable State. Jossey-Bass. San Francisco, CA.
334. Schory, M.E. 1990. "Whole Language and the Speech Language Pathologists in Language, Speech and Hearing Services in Schools." 21, pp. 206-211.
335. Schuster, D.H. 1985. "A Critical Review of American Foreign Language Studies Using Suggestopaedia." Paper delivered at the Aimav Linguistic Conference at the University of Nijmegen, The Netherlands.
336. Schwartz, J.M. & Begley, S. 2002. The Mind and the Brain: Neuroplasticity and the power of mental force. Regan Books/Harper Collins. NY.
337. Scruggs, E. & Brigham, J. 1987. "The Challenges of Metacognitive Instruction." RASE. 11 (6), pp. 16-18.
338. Seaward, B. L. 1996. Health and Wellness Journal Workbook.
339. Segerstrom, S.C. & Miller, G.E. 2004. "Psychological Stress and the Human Immune System: A meta-analytic study of 30 years of inquiry." Psychological Bulletin Vol. 130. N04. 601-630.
340. Shapiro, R.B., Champagne, V.G. & De Costa, D. 1988. "The Speech-language Pathologist: Consultant to the classroom educator." Reading Improvement. 25 (1), pp. 2-9.
341. Sheth, B.R. 2006. "Practice Makes Imperfect: Restorative effects of sleep on motor learning." Society for Neuroscience. Program 14-14.
342. Simon, C.S. 1987. "Out of the Broom Closet and into the Classroom: The Emerging SLP." Journal of Childhood Communication Disorders. 11 (1-2), pp. 81-90.
343. Singer, T. 2004. "How Your Brain Handles Love and Pain." http://www.msnbc.msn.com/id/4313263.
344. Sizer, T.R. 1984. Horacel's Compromise: The dilemma of the American high school. Houghton Mifflin. Boston, MA.
345. Slabbert, J. 1989. "Metalearning as the Most Essential Aim in Education for All." Paper presented at University of Pretoria, Faculty of Education. Pretoria, SA.
346. Sleep. 2003. http://www.applesforhealth.com/lacksleep1.html.
347. Slife, B.D., Weiss, J. & Bell, T. 1985. "Separability of Metacognition and Cognition: Problem solving in learning disabled and regular students." Journal of Educational Psychology. 77 (4), pp. 437-445.
348. Smith, A. 1999. Accelerated Learning in Practice. Network Educational Press. Stafford, UK.
349. Sperry, R. 1968. "Hemisphere Disconnection and Unity in Conscious Awareness." American Psychologist. 23 (1968).
350. Solms, M. 1999. http://www.abc.net.au/rn/talks/8.30/helthrpt/stories/s44369.htm.
351. Solms, M. 2000. "Forebrain Mechanisms of Dreaming are Activated from a Variety of Sources." Behavioral and Brain Sciences. 23 (6): 1035-1040; 1083-1121.
352. Solms, M. 1997. "The Neuropsychology of Dreams: A clinico-anatomical study." Lawrence Erlbaum.
353. Spitz, R. 1983. http://www.pep-web.org/document.php?id=PPSY.002.0181A.
354. Springer, S.P. & Deutsch, G. 1998. Left Brain, Right Brain. W.H. Freeman & Company. NY.
355. Stengel, R. 2009. Ed. TIME Your Brain: A User' Guide. TIME Books. Des Moines, IA.
356. Stephan, K.M., Fink, G.R. et al. 1995. "Functional Anatomy of Mental Representation of Upper Extremity Movements in Healthy Subjects." Journal of Neurophysiology. 73(1): 373-86.
357. Sternberg, R. 1979. "The Nature of Mental Abilities." American Psychologist. 34, pp. 214-230.
358. Stickgold, R., Hobson, R. et al. 2001. "Sleep, Learning, and Dreams: Offline memory reprocessing." Science. 294 (554): 1052-57.

359. Stickgold, R. & Wehrwein, P. 2009. "Sleep Now, Remember Later." Newsweek. http:/www.newsweek.com/id/194650.
360. Stress in Children. www.cookchildrens.org.
361. Sylwester, R. 1985. "Research on Memory: Major discoveries, major educational challenges." Educational Leadership. pp. 69-75.
362. Szyf, Moshe. Epigenetics. 2009. http://www.the-scientist.com/article/display/55843/.
363. Tattershall, S. 1987. "Mission Impossible: Learning how a classroom works before it's too late!" Journal of Childhood Communication Disorders. 11 (1), pp. 181-184.
364. Taub, E., Uswatte, G. et al. 2005. "Use of CI Therapy for Plegic Hands after Chronic Stroke." Presentation at the Society for neuroscience. Washington D.C.
365. Taubes, G. 2008. Good Calories, Bad Calories: Fats, carbs and the controversial science of diet and health. Anchor Books. NY.
366. Thembela, A. 1990. "Education for Blacks in South Africa: Issues, problems and perspectives." Journal of the Society for Accelerative Learning and Teaching. 15 (12), pp. 45-57.
367. Thurman, S.K. & Widerstrom, A.H. 1990. Infants and Young Children with Special Needs: A developmental and ecological approach, 2nd Ed. Paul H. Brookes. Baltimore, MD.
368. Tunajek, S. 2006. "The Attitude Factor." http://www.aana.com/uploadedFiles/Resources/Wellness/nb_milestone_0406.pdf.
369. "Understanding the Different Types of Depression." 2002. www.Depression-Anxiety.com.
370. Uys, I.C. 1989. "Single Case Experimental Designs: An essential service in communicatively disabled care." The South African Journal of Communication Disorders. 36, pp. 53-59.
371. Van derVyfer, D.W. 1985. "SALT in South Africa: Needs and parameters." Journal of the Society for Accelerative Learning and Teaching. 10(3), pp. 187-200.
372. Van derVyver, D.W. & de Capdeville, B. 1990. "Towards the Mountain: Characteristics and implications of the South African UPPTRAIL pilot project." Journal of the Society for Accelerative Learning and Teaching. 15 (1 & 2), pp. 59-74.
373. Vaughan, S.C. 1997. The Talking Cure: The science behind psychotherapy. Grosset/Putnam. NY.
374. Vaynman S., & Gomez-Pinilla. 2005. "License to Run: Exercise impacts functional plasticity in the intact and injured central nervous system by using neurotrophins." Neurorehabilitation and Neural Repair. 19(4): 283-95.
375. Von Bertalanaffy, L. 1968. General Systems Theory. Braziller. NY.
376. Vythilingam, M. & Heim, C. "Childhood Trauma Associated with Smaller Hippocampal Volume in Women with Major Depression." American Journal of Psychiatry. 159(12): 2072-80.
377. Walker, M.P. & Stickgold, R. 2006. "Sleep, Memory and Plasticity." Annual Review of Psychology.
378. Wark, D.M. 1986. "Using Imagery to Teach Study Skills." Journal of the Society for Accelerative Learning and Teaching. 11 (3), pp. 203-220.
379. Waterland, R.A. & Jirtle, R.L. 2003. "Transposable Elements: Targets for early nutritional effects on epigenetic gene regulation." Molecular and Cellular Biology. 23(15): 5293-5300.
380. Wenger, W. 1985. "An Example of Limbic Learning." Journal of the Society for Accelerative Learning and Teaching. 10 (1), pp. 51-68.
381. Wertsch, J.V. 1985. Culture, Communication and Cognitions. NY.
382. Whitelson, S. 1985. "The Brain Connection: The corpus callosum is larger in left-handers." Science. 229, pp. 665-8.
383. Widener, C. 2004. The Angel Inside. E Books. www.theangelinside.com.
384. Wilson, R.S., Mendes, C.F. et al. 2002. "Participation in Cognitively Stimulating Activities and Risk of Incident in Alzheimer's Disease." JAMA. 287(6): 742-48.
385. Witelson, S.F., Kigar, D.L. & Harvey, T. 1999. "The Exceptional Brain of Albert Einstein." Lancet. 353:2149-53.
386. Wright, N.H. 2005. Finding Freedom from Your Fears. Fleming H. Revell. Grand Rapids, MI.
387. Wurtman, J. 1986. Managing Your Mind-Mood through Food. Harper/Collins. NY.
388. Zaborszky, L. 2002. "The Modular Organization of Brain Systems: Basal forebrain; the last frontier. Changing views of Cajal's neuron." Progressing Brain Research. (136) 359-372.
389. Zaidel, E. 1985. "Roger Sperry: An Appreciation." in Benson, D.F. & Zaidel, E. (Eds.). The Dual Brain. The Guilford Press. NY.
390. Zakaluk, B.L. & Klassen, M. 1992. "Enhancing the Performance of a High School Student Labelled Learning Disabled." Journal of Reading. 36 (1).
391. Zdenek, M. 1983. The Right Brain Experience. McGraw-Hill. GB.
392. Zimmerman, B.J. & Schunk, D.H. 1989. Self-Regulated Learning and Academic Achievement: Theory, research and practice. Springer-Verby. NY.